pocket
Guy Andrews
ROAD BIKE
maintenance

D0420031

Note
While every effort has been made to ensure that the content of this book
is as technically accurate and as sound as possible, neither the author nor
the publishers can accept responsibility for any injury or loss sustained as
a result of the use of this material.

Published by Bloomsbury Publishing Plc
50 Bedford Square
London WC1B 3DP
www.bloomsbury.com

First edition 2014

ISBN (print): 978 1 4081 7098 4

A CIP catalogue record for this book is available from the British Library.

Cover photographs © Gerard Brown
Inside photographs © Gerard Brown
Designed by Jonathan Briggs

This book is produced using paper that is made from wood grown in
managed, sustainable forests. It is natural, renewable and recyclable.
The logging and manufacturing processes conform to the environmental
regulations of the country of origin.

Printed and bound in China by Hung Hing Printing Group Limited
10 9 8 7 6 5 4 3 2 1

■ CONTENTS

Preface

Many cyclists are nervous about working on their own bike, but nearly everyone has the basic ability to look after a bicycle. All the parts are readily accessible and the majority of jobs need only simple tools.

The aim with *Pocket Road Bike Maintenance* has been to distil the most useful information and most common jobs into a compact volume that can live in your toolbox or pannier. The key aspects of road bike maintenance are covered here, so you'll have all the basic information you need to keep your bike in good shape, make straightforward adjustments and fixes and sort out problems that may arise when you are out on the road.

Every cyclist should be able to work on their own bike, even if it's just the simple things. Hopefully this book will give you the confidence to have a go.

Acknowledgements

A big thank you to photographer, Gerard Brown; to designer, Jonathan Briggs – who had a hell of a job on his hands; and to the ever-patient Sarah Cole, Lisa Thomas and everyone at Bloomsbury.

I'd also like to thank:
Phil, Gill and Roger at Mosquito Bikes for Independent Fabrication and Pegoretti bikes, many thanks all.
Chris Garrison for Wrench Force tools, Bontrager wheels and Trek bikes.
Jordan Gibbons and everyone at Rouleur magazine.
Rory Hitchens and Dom Mason at Upgrade Bikes for Lezyne and other such lovely stuff they do.
Shelley Childs at Continental for tyres, tubes and tubulars.
Chris Snook and Albert Steward at Madison for Shimano and Park Tools.
Grant Young at Condor Cycles.
Barry Scott at Bespoke.
Michel Lethenet at Mavic.
Cedric Chicken and Mike Catlin at Chicken Cycle Kit for Mavic wheels, Campagnolo, Cinelli, Tifosi and Time bikes.
Joshua Riddle at Campagnolo.
And to Taz.

Whether you are an experienced racer or just starting out, knowing how to keep your bike in peak condition is essential to your enjoyment of cycling. Being able to recognise the early warning signs of mechanical trouble – and what to do about them – means less time and money wasted getting your bike fixed and more time in the saddle. Whatever rider or mechanic level you are at, we hope that this compact book will help. It covers all the most common maintenance and repair tasks, all clearly illustrated. Fixing a bike for yourself is hugely rewarding and it's great to know that you can be miles from home and yet be able to fix your bike in the unlikely event of a mechanical failure.

TYPES OF BIKE

The term "road bike" covers a wide variety of styles of bike, each designed for a slightly different purpose.

ROAD RACING BIKE

This is a road bike similar to the ones professional riders use. Road racing geometry is very aggressive and the position is quite extreme. Professional riders spend a long time in the saddle and are used to an aerodynamic position, so this will not be suited to a rider that only manages to ride a couple of times a week. Be realistic with your aspirations and consider a bike with a more

"Sportive" approach. Many manufacturers now offer road bikes with the same technology and componentry as the professional bike but with a more relaxed fit and usually a more comfortable ride. Many of these frames are ideal for long days in the saddle and riding over rough terrain and poor road surfaces.

CYCLO-CROSS BIKE

The sport of cyclo-cross involves racing road-style bikes off-road on grass, mud, sand or snow. Cyclo-cross is a tough sport and teaches skill and technique that will help your road riding improve. Specialist cyclo-cross bikes have clearance for 35mm knobbly tyres, with either cantilever or, increasingly, disc brakes. Pure 'cross bikes lack any frame fittings for racks, mudguards or even bottles (races are only an hour long), but most

manufacturers make cyclo-cross bikes to which accessories can be fitted, and these make versatile commuter/winter training/off-road bikes.

TOURING

Touring bikes are designed for carrying luggage and comfort for long rides. They're usually made from steel, with slightly more relaxed angles than a race bike. The wheelbase is usually longer, too, with longer chainstays partly for comfort and partly so that your heels clear rear panniers. Cantilever brakes are common on tourers, giving clearance for large tyres and mudguards.

TRACK

Track bikes are purist machines for racing on banked velodromes. They have fixed gears and no brakes. Geometry is steep with short rake forks and a high bottom bracket (for pedal and banking clearance). Track bikes also have niche set-ups and types too – sprinters prefer stiff, over-built frames with steel handlebars and lower front ends while pursuit bikes have aero riding positions like road time trial bikes.

WINTER BIKE

The Northern European weather is hardly the ideal environment for bicycles. Winter bikes are often an entry-level bike or perhaps a retired racing bike. But seeing as most of your long training miles will be on this bike, a specialist bike with mudguards is the best way. Use the same set-up as your race bike, and similar contact points (saddle, bars, pedals), to prevent injury and discomfort.

TIME TRIAL BIKE

Time trials, with individual riders racing against the clock, are the pivotal stages of big races like the Tour de France and the Giro d'Italia. If you're taking your time trial riding seriously, you'll want to get a specific time trial bike. A TT bike will have steeper frame angles, placing the rider further forwards in a more powerful pedalling position. Aero bars and wheels cut drag but add weight.

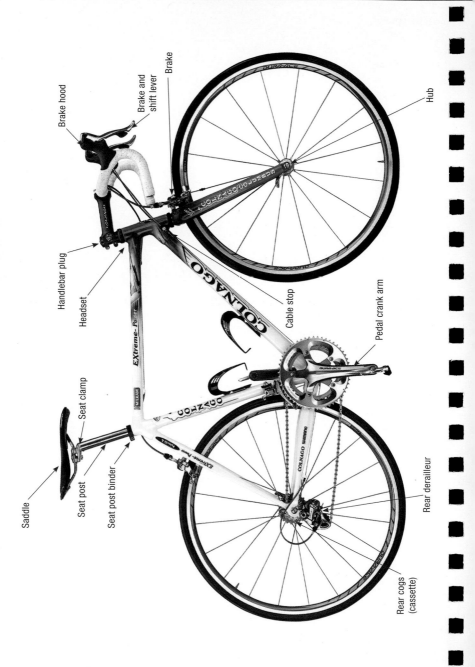

Brake hood

Brake and shift lever

Brake

Hub

Handlebar plug

Headset

Cable stop

Pedal crank arm

Seat clamp

Saddle

Seat post

Seat post binder

Rear derailleur

Rear cogs (cassette)

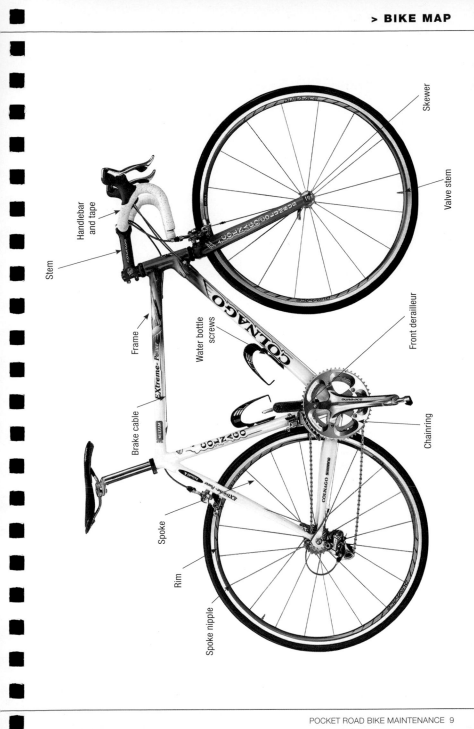

Skewer

Valve stem

Handlebar and tape

Stem

Front derailleur

Frame

Water bottle screws

Chainring

Brake cable

Spoke

Rim

Spoke nipple

BUYING A BIKE

Good entry-level road bikes usually cost around £500 to £800. Because this is a very competitive price point these bikes are often very good value, featuring quality parts and a well-made frame. However, entry-level bikes are not designed and built to be pushed to the limits, so as your riding improves you'll probably want to upgrade what you ride. Your main priorities are the frame and forks, then the wheels, then the contact points (saddle, handlebars and pedals), and lastly the components. Components are last on the list because they'll wear out in time and, should you want to upgrade them, you can do it when they wear out. The frame, forks and wheels are always the most expensive parts of a bike, so look for the manufacturers that put the most effort into these areas.

BIKE BUYING TIPS

1 Take an experienced cycling friend with you to give you advice. Research the brands you like the look of. Phone the manufacturers for catalogues and take a balanced view, and use the internet.

2 Buy a range of up-to-date magazines to consider your options. Find back issues of group tests of bikes in your price range, or even e-mail the magazine to ask their opinion.

3 Although you can buy bikes by mail order, it's best to visit a bike shop in person. You'll be able to try a variety of bikes out for size, take them for test rides and be pointed in the right direction by experienced staff. Your new bike will also be set up properly from the start.

4 Consider that you'll need after-sales support, so you'll need to build loyalty with the shop. Don't just buy cheaper elsewhere and then expect a local dealer to fix or deal with the warranty on your new bike for free. It's always worth thinking about buying some extras (helmet, clothing, tools and so on) when you're at the shop buying your bike. This is probably the most you'll spend in the shop at one time, so they may well offer you a few incentives, even if it's just a free bottle and an inner tube.

5 Don't be lured by discounted bikes, special offers or ex-demonstration bikes unless you're absolutely sure it's the bike for you and it's the right size.

6 If the shop doesn't have your size, wait until they can get one. It's better to leave it a little longer and have the right bike.

7 Always ask local cyclists for recommendations and ask them about the local shops – for example, which one is good for advice and which one specialises in particular brands? It's always better to go to a dealer who has a good reputation. Ask lots of questions in the shop and make sure they have a good mechanic and a well-equipped (preferably tidy) workshop. As discussed, they should also offer you a free first service and warranty back-up.

You should always buy good-quality tools, as you'll use them to fix lots of bikes. Specialist bike tools are expensive, but they make complicated procedures a breeze, and will also ensure you don't damage your new components and your bike or hurt yourself. Bodging jobs with cheap tools only ends in compromise, and if you have a good-quality bike it deserves the tools to complement it.

WORKSHOP TOOL KIT

For a modest outlay you can cover most home workshop jobs. Some specialist tools do cost a fair amount, but in time you will consider them a worthwhile investment. In the meantime, the best advice is to buy components from a local shop and get their mechanic to fit them for you if you don't have the tools yourself. As you become a more competent mechanic you may want to consider how much you spend in the bike workshop compared to how much the tools will cost you. These basic tools will cover most jobs other than frame preparation, headset installation and wheel building.

- Allen keys: 1.5mm, 2mm, 2.5mm, 3mm, 4mm, 5mm, 6mm, 8mm and 10mm are the sizes most often used

- Track pump

- Chain cleaner

- Cleaning brushes

- Pliers (flat and needle nose)

- Cable cutters

- Screwdrivers (small and large; flat and cross-head)

- Nylon hammer (or mallet) and ball-peen (metal-working) hammer

- A set of metric, open-ended spanners from 6mm to 24mm

- Cassette lock ring tool

- Chain whip

- Chain tool

- Cable puller

- "Podger" (sharp-ended tool like a bradawl)

- Star nut-setting tool

- Adjustable spanner

- Cone spanners (17mm,15mm and 13mm)

- Pedal spanner

- Workshop-quality chain tool

- Chain checker (for measuring chain wear)

- Torque wrenches

- Crank-removing tool

- Bottom bracket tools

- Headset spanners (optional)

- Wheel-truing stand

- Spoke keys

- Hacksaw (standard and junior)

- Files (flat and half-round)

- Socket set

THE TOOLS

1. Tool box
2. Long-nose pliers
3. Allen keys
4. Chainring nut spanner
5. Chain tool
6. Screw drivers
7. Chain whip
8. Pedal spanner
9. Cone spanners
10. Chain wear tool
11. Crank remover
12. Adjustable spanner
13. Cassette tool
14. Cable cutters
15. Tyre levers
16. Wheel jig
17. Crank bolt spanner
18. Torque wrench
19. Multitool
20. Shimano Bottom Bracket tool
21. Star-fangled nut setter
22. Crank remover
23. Cassette tool
24. Cable puller
25. Spanner
26. Headset spanners
27. Cable pliers
28. Soft mallet

WORKSHOP SET-UP

A home workshop is a bit of a luxury, but fixing your bike in the kitchen is never a great idea. So here are some tips for setting up your workshop at home. A stable workstand (below) is essential. The best type is fixed to a wall or a solid workbench, so jobs that require bashing or heavy leaning won't make the stand move around the floor as you "dance" with your bike. A tool board helps you find tools quickly, and quality tools should be stored in a toolbox especially if your workshop is damp. You can also assemble an "in the field" toolbox that you can take with you to races or rides so you can fix emergencies in the car park.

If you do have to fix your bike in the house, you'll need something on the floor to soak up the mess. Workshop mats are readily available from bike or tool shops. They're a good idea in a dedicated workshop too, and will keep your feet warm in the winter.

Hooks and lockable anchor points are a good idea, just in case you're broken into. Storing your bike(s) like this also prevents them from falling over and getting scratched by the lawn mower.

WORKSHOP PRACTICES

HEALTH AND SAFETY WARNING

Lubricants, disc brake fluid, degreasers and bike washes look after your bike, but they can be very harmful to your skin – always read the instructions and labels on cans before you start work. Take care and use appropriate personal protective equipment when working on your bike. Latex or nitrile gloves and workshop aprons are a great idea, and safety glasses are a must when using release agents or operating grinders and drills.

READ THE INSTRUCTIONS

This may seem obvious, but it's very important. Warranties and guarantees are only any good if you install things correctly. Even the simplest of components will have some recommendations from the manufacturer – so stick to them. Use the recommended tools and torque settings. If in doubt, contact the shop or the manufacturer. Don't make expensive mistakes.

WORKSHOP EQUIPMENT

VICE

The vice needs to be properly bolted and secured to the solid workbench. A vice is essential for hub and headset jobs, and a pair of replaceable "soft jaws" for the vice will help to protect valuable and sensitive components.

WHEEL JIG

Your wheel jig should preferably be bench-mounted. A solid wheel jig makes truing wheels far easier. If you intend to learn how to build wheels, or just want to get better at home truing, then a wheel jig is a must-have item.

TORQUE WRENCHES

Torque wrenches make it easy to fasten bolts to manufacturers' recommended figures. They're simple to use – set the level on the screw gauge on the handle, shown in Newton metres (Nm), then add the correct Allen or bolt head and tighten the bolt until the handle "gives" with a click. This type is perfect for most Allen bolts on a bike. You'll need a small torque wrench for things like stem and handlebar bolts and a larger one for cassette lock rings and bottom brackets.

TRACK PUMP

A floor-standing track pump will set tyre pressures quickly and accurately and is far better than a mini pump. However, some pressure gauges are more reliable than others, so get a separate, accurate tyre-pressure gauge too.

LUBRICANTS

You'll develop preferences for particular brands of lubes and greases, but the modern bicycle requires a selection of advanced lubricants to keep it running sweetly:

- **Ti-prep (or copper slip)** – a grease with tiny copper flakes in it, which prevents titanium and alloys from seizing – must be used on all titanium threads.

- **Anti-seize grease** – this is for large threads and components that stay put for long periods (seat posts, bottom bracket threads, headset cups and pedal threads).

- **PTFE (Teflon)-based light dry lube** – this is preferred for summer use and assemblies like mechs and brake calliper pivots.

- **Heavy wet lube** – this is best for wet weather as it's harder to wash away than dry lube.

- **Silicone greases** – use these for intricate moving parts like pedal and hub bearings.

- **Waterproof greases** – use these for components that get ignored for long periods like Aheadset bearings.

- **Degreaser** – used for cleaning moving parts and components that get bunged up with muck.

- **Bike wash** – use it for tyres, frame tubes and saddles.

- **Release agent** – this is good for removing seized seat-posts and stubborn bottom brackets. Be careful, as it can ruin your paintwork.

CLEANING YOUR BIKE

To keep your bike running smoothly and ensure that the components will last, wash your bike at least once a week – especially in the winter. Washing your bike is a great way to get close to it and inspect every aspect of its workings. Wear some wellies, rubber gloves and waterproof clothing, as you'll then be able to concentrate on the job properly. Find a suitable area to clean your bike. You'll need plenty of water and the by-products from washing a bike can be quite messy – a concrete area with a water supply and a drain is best. Always clean the floor with a stiff brush when you've finished, as the degreasing fluids can make the floor very slippery.

1 Always clean the under-side of the saddle and the seat post first, so you can place the bike into the workstand before you wash the rest of your bike (most work-stand clamps hold the seat post), and also because it's best to start at the top of the bike and work down so you don't get muck on stuff you've already washed.

2 Once the bike is in the stand, drop both of the wheels out, as they're far easier to clean when they're out of the bike. Insert a chain roller to hold the chain in place. This will also help you clean the chain, let you rotate the chain and cranks easily, and keep the chain out of the way as you wash the rest of the bike.

3 Use a spray-on de-greaser. You can dilute these cleaning sprays with water, as they tend to be quite concentrated and powerful. Be careful to read the instructions, as these fluids can be caustic and affect the finish of your bike. Most are not too kind to your hands either, so it's best to wear rubber gloves.

▶

4 Brush the whole drive train with stronger degreaser solution. The citrus stuff is usually best for this. Work into the gear mechanisms and the chain rings, and leave it to penetrate for a few minutes.

5 Clean the chain. Use plenty of strong degreaser and a small, stiff brush. Work carefully all the way around the chain, making sure you clean both sides and inside the plates.

6 You can also use a chain-cleaner – a brush is more thorough, but the cleaner is quicker and less messy. They're good for cleaning the chain without washing the whole bike. Regular re-lubing on a clean chain will prevent the build-up of grime and will lengthen the life of your gear components.

7 Use a big brush to clean the chainrings and cranks. You'll need to re-apply degreaser several times to remove all the road dirt and oil residue. Keep scrubbing until it has all gone.

8 Use a sponge and plenty of water to wash off any detergent and solvents from the drivetrain. Clean out the pedals and the shoe cleats using a smaller, toothbrush-size brush. Keep the pedal springs well lubricated and check their tension regularly.

9 Then you can start to clean the wheels. Clean the cassette first. Again, a strong degreaser is best, as it'll shift the greasy black stuff faster. Use a sprocket cleaner, stiff brush or strip of fabric to clean between the sprockets. Clean and inspect the hubs too.

10 Use a milder degreaser on the tyres and rims. Soak the rims and tyres, and leave for a moment. Once the road and brake dirt starts to lift, scrub the tyres and rims thoroughly with a stiff brush and lots of water. Once they're clean, rinse completely with clean water and dry off with a rag.

11 Remove any debris from the slots in the brake pads and clean the brake mechanisms – use a pointed implement to push out any road grit and brake pad dust. Wash the brakes and pads with a sponge and be careful not to mis-align the calliper as you clean.

12 Be careful when cleaning the gear shifters and brake levers – don't spray degreaser directly on the seals, and clean them with a rag rather than a stiff brush. Spraying water and degreaser into the internals will cause problems in the future.

13 Finally, lubricate the chain with a suitable lube and use a light spray-lube on any gear and brake pivots (not the brake shoes or pads though!). Rub away any lube residue from the chain with a clean cloth. Give the paint a buff with some frame polish and a duster. Inspect the frame for damage and make sure that all the components are dry and free from degreaser residue.

PRO CLEANING TIPS

1   Always work at a good height and use a solid workstand – it saves your back and means you'll take more care over the washing.

2   When it's wet always wash your bikes immediately after a ride, as once all the road dirt and grime is dry the bike is far harder to clean.

3   Keep the degreaser close to hand – perhaps in an old bottle in the bottle cage – as this saves time and avoids waste.

While specialist track and time trial bikes often sport carbon fibre three or four-spoke wheels, or full carbon discs, the vast majority of bikes still use wire-spoked wheels. For most purposes, it's impossible to beat the combination of stiffness, low weight and serviceability of spoked wheels. Many wheels are now factory built with proprietary hubs and spokes, rather than assembled from off-the-shelf components, but the principles are the same.

REMOVING WHEELS

The standard road-bike wheel has a quick-release (QR) mechanism which is excellent for removing the wheels instantly – great for repairing punctures, quick racing-wheel changes, or putting your bike in the back of your car. But a QR mechanism can be potentially hazardous if done up incorrectly. On most bikes the front-wheel system has a slightly different technique from the rear-wheel system. If you're removing both wheels, take the front one out first – this will make the bike easier to manage and means that you won't have to drag the chain and gears on the ground.

FRONT WHEELS

1 "Lawyer tabs" are so called because of several well-publicised US lawsuits in the early days of the mountain bike, when a few companies were sued over front wheels dropping out of the forks unannounced, which had catastrophic results. They're designed to prevent the wheel from falling out should the QR lever be done up too loosely.

2 Once the QR is undone the wheel may still not drop out completely, so the nut on the non-lever side needs to be loosened a little more. The key here is to remember how much you've undone it and not to remove it completely. To clear the tabs, undo the nut – three full turns will be enough on most bikes. The wheel will then drop out.

3 To replace the wheel, position the axle into the fork ends – the springs on the inside of the QR mechanism help centralise the nut and the lever, making this easier. Replace the wheels with the bike on the ground so that the weight of the bike ensures that the axle is fully engaged. Retighten the QR nut and push the lever fully home.

REAR WHEELS

1 The chain should be on the smallest sprocket (or cog) and the largest chain ring, so make sure you change into this gear before you start. This makes it easier to get the chain off the cassette and easier to replace the wheel afterwards.

3 The wheel will remain trapped into the bike by the chain, so twist the mech backwards to release the wheel. The chain should stay on the front chain wheel, so it'll be easier if you start with the chain in this position when you replace the wheel. The wheel will now easily come out of the rear triangle.

2 Stand behind the bike and hold the bike upright with your legs trapping the wheel, leaving your hands free to remove the wheel. Now undo the lever.

4 To replace the rear wheel, the mech needs to be sprung into the correct position with the wheel in the bike. Next, wrap the chain over the top of the smallest sprocket to help the wheel slot into the dropouts.

5 Pull the wheel upwards and backwards, and it should slot into place easily. If it doesn't, the wheel may have become snagged on the brake pads, or the mech may not be in the correct gear position.

6 Don't adjust the nut on the QR lever, as the rear wheel should clear the dropouts and slip in easily. However, it's worth checking that the lever feels tight as it closes. Rest your weight on the bike, as this will keep the wheel central in the rear dropouts.

DOING UP THE QR LEVER (BOTH WHEELS)

1 Once the wheel is slotted into the dropouts (or fork ends), slowly tighten the nut up until the lever starts to tighten at this position. This is when the cam on the mechanism begins to "bite" and when the wheel hub is gripped across the lock nuts and by the fork ends.

2 The lever should close firmly, needing enough effort so that you have to use your thumb and press hard. Any harder and you'll struggle to undo it again. Check that the wheel spins centrally in the forks or rear stays and you're safe to ride.

TRUING WHEELS

Wheels go out of true due to broken or loose spokes. A wheel is like a suspension bridge, and any imbalance in the supports (spokes) places more stress on the neighbouring supports. Spin the wheel and see where the buckles are and where the wheel has uneven tension. It should sit centrally in the jig (or bike frame if you're out riding). Your job is to find out where, and more importantly how, the wheel is being pulled away from this centre line. Don't attempt to true a wheel until you've a good idea what is causing the buckle.

Lateral (side-to-side) buckles are the easiest to solve:

- if the wheel hops to the left, tighten the spoke on the right or loosen the spoke on the left;

- if the wheel hops to the right, tighten the spoke on the left or loosen the spoke on the right.

However, radial (up-and-down) buckles are a little different:

- if the hop is towards the hub, the spoke is too tight;

- if the hop is away from the hub, the spoke is too loose.

So, if the rim hops to the left and towards the hub at the same time, there's a spoke pulling too tightly on the left, and if the rim hops to the right and away from the hub at the same time, there's a loose spoke on the right. Remember to make small adjustments at first – no more than a quarter- or half-turn.

Rear wheels have tighter spokes on the drive side than they do on the non-drive side. The non-drive spokes are also longer. This means that they require fewer turns than the drive side – it depends on the wheel, but the ratio is about 2:1. On front hubs you'll always need to loosen or tighten the same amount on both sides.

1 The usual cause of a buckle is a broken spoke – however, here we are trying to find the loose ones that may just require tightening. Grab several spokes at a time and squeeze them to feel where the problem loose areas are before you start to true the wheel.

2 Always use a spoke key that fits the nipples snugly. A loose-fitting key will ruin the nipple very easily, especially if the nipple is tight. Spokes tighten with a standard right-hand thread, so if you're using your right hand you'll need to turn the spoke key towards you to tighten the spoke and away from you to loosen it.

3 A severe radial hop or a skip in the rim can signify a set or group of very loose or tight spokes. Try to find the loose ones first. Then, using quarter-turns only, adjust the tension in two or four spokes at a time on each side (shown here with the red and black spoke keys) – you need to pull on both sides equally to prevent the wheel going out laterally as well as radially.

4 "Dish" describes the shape of the wheel. The rim needs to be centred in the frame for the bike to handle properly. Wheel dish is determined by measuring the wheel with a dishing stick, which checks that the lock nuts are equally spaced on either side of the rim. Dish guarantees that the wheels will run in line and also allows for efficient braking.

5 Accurate truing has to be done using a quality wheel jig rather than with the wheel still in the bike. Wheel jigs provide more stability, so the wheel doesn't rock around when you spin it, and adjustable guides. If you have to true a wheel in the frame on a ride, be sure to finish it properly when you get home.

6 Professional wheel builders will use a spoke tension meter. This can accurately measure spoke tension and enables a good wheelbuilder to keep variation in spoke tension to around 10 per cent. This is also useful when truing a wheel, as you can assess which spokes are being pushed too hard and are therefore likely to break first.

7 Once you're happy that the wheel is perfectly round again, carefully "stress" it in your lap or gently on the floor. Don't stress the wheel with your full weight, especially if the bearings are sealed as they're vulnerable to side loads. You'll hear the wheel click and ping as the spokes find their position. This may mean that the rim moves a little, so double-check it in the jig before you're finished.

8 Finally, replace the rim tape. I always use tape that will stick to the rim – this way you know it won't come loose and move around under the tube. Plastic tape is better than cloth, as cloth tape holds water and will rust the eyelets, which In turn can seize the nipples. Rim tape should be renewed every time rims are removed – never re-use old tape.

REPLACING SPOKES

1 If the head of the spoke faces into the hub centre (outbound), you'll have to thread the spoke in from the opposite side of the wheel. Spokes cross three times between the hub and the rim, either crossing under twice and over once, or over twice and under once. Either way, it's essential that you copy this lacing to maintain the integrity and strength of the wheel.

2 The spoke can pass through the lower part of the spokes on the opposite side of the wheel. However, lacing is trickier if the head of the spoke faces out from the hub centre (inbound). You have to angle the spoke upwards so that it avoids the crossing at the other side of the wheel. Be careful not to bend the spoke too much and weaken it.

3 In order to lace the spoke around the rim, you'll have to push it under the rim. Bend the spoke very gently and evenly so that it can tuck under the rim. The correct-length spoke will meet the rim eyelet and should be long enough to pass through the nipple and be level with the top of it on the inside of the rim. Any longer and the spoke will be too slack on the nipple.

4 Take up the slack with a screwdriver (or nipple-driver as shown here) before you start to true the wheel. Make a note of how far the other spokes protrude from the nipple and – if you have the correct-length spoke – you can get the spoke to a similar position.

SERVICING CUP-AND-CONE HUBS

Cup-and-cone hubs with loose bearings are very simple to service. The first few times it can be challenging, but experience really speeds the process up. The key is to make sure that all the components are in top condition – any wear and tear to the cones or bearings means that the parts should be replaced. Most Shimano road hubs, from Tiagra to Dura Ace, use the same principle and many older Campagnolo hubs also follow the same pattern. Most contemporary Campagnolo hubs from Mirage to Record have an oversized aluminium axle and a system that requires no specialist cone spanners or tools. They have several specific parts but are simple to adjust, and everything is replaceable and serviceable.

FRONT HUBS

1 The key to easy hub servicing is only working on one side. If you keep one side intact, the factory setting spacing over the lock nuts is easier to retain. All front hubs measure 100mm over the lock nuts – this measurement is critical so that the wheel can easily be replaced in the forks.

2 Undo and remove the lock nut, the washer and, finally, the cone. Cone spanners are very thin and flat. This means that they can fit into the machined flats on the sides of the cone and can adjust and tighten the cones without snagging on the washer and lock nut. Use the correct size (and don't use cone spanners to remove your pedals, as this will damage them!). Hold the cone with a cone spanner and release the lock nut with a 17mm spanner.

3 The cone is made from hardened steel and has a highly polished bearing surface. Inspect the cone carefully for any rough patches on the surface – this is known as pitting. On most front wheels there's only a cone, washer and lock nut.

▶

4 Remove the cone, spacers and – very carefully – the axle. I find it's best to do this over something that will catch the bearings should they fall out – at least place your hand over the end. Place the threaded components down on the workbench in the order they came off the hub to help you remember the order to return them in. Clean the axle and cones, leaving one side on the axle and in one piece.

5 Keep all the old bearings so that you can check you're replacing the same size and quantity. It's good practice to replace the bearings after every strip-down. The bearings are slightly more vulnerable than the cones and the hub surfaces, so they tend to wear out first. Look at them closely and you'll see tiny potholes. Bearings need to be mirror-finished, so if they're even slightly dull they need replacing. It's useful to have a magnetic screwdriver for this job, as it'll make re-installation far easier. Store spare bearings on a magnet to make them easier to manage.

6 Clean the inside of the bearing surfaces and inspect for damage. If the bearing surfaces and cones are pitted, you'll need to replace either the cones or the hub assembly. Replacing the cones and the bearings, and resetting them in grease, will usually solve any hub roughness.

7 To grease the hub cups properly, you don't have to remove the hub seals – they're factory fitted and are very hard to replace properly, as they're pressed into the shell of the hub, and it's possible to see into the hub with the seals in place. However, if you do have to remove them, be very careful. Wrap a rag around a tyre lever and prise the seals out carefully. Don't use a screwdriver as this can bend the seal, and if that happens you'll never get it back in again. To replace the seal, use your fingers to locate it and then tap it home using a rubber mallet.

8 When all the bearings are installed, take the loose cone and push it back into the hub. Rotate it a couple of times to seat the bearings. This will also tell you if there's any damage to the bearing surface inside the hub, and will stick the bearings in place so you can turn the wheel over to do the other side. Next, double-check that there are the right amount of bearings in the hub. Lastly, smear a little more grease on top of the bearings and check there isn't any grease inside the hub. You'll then be able to push the axle through without making a big mess.

9 Replace the axle (remember to return it the same way round as it was at removal). As you've only disturbed one set of bearings, the spacing won't have been altered. Screw the cone onto the axle and up to the bearings.

10 Spin the axle in your fingers and "rock it slightly from side to side – you're looking for the point at which there's no "play", only smooth spinning. When you're happy that the bearings are running smoothly, replace the washer and then the lock nut. At this stage they need to be finger-tight.

11 With practice, you'll be able to set the cones like this and simply do up the cone as in step 2. However, when you tighten the lock nut for the last time, you may also either loosen the cone slightly or tighten it. Most hubs have seals in the hub body that will drag a little when the cone is set. To set the cones properly you'll need two cone spanners (13mm for front hubs) – with two spanners you can work the cones against each other. So, if you over-tighten the lock nut, place the two cone spanners on either side of the hub and slightly undo the cones until the axle spins freely.

REAR HUBS

1 Remove the cassette using a chain whip and a cassette-removing tool. This will allow you to access the cones that are obscured by the cassette sprockets and lockring.

2 Undo the lock nut and cone as per front hubs, making sure to work on the non-drive side. Leave the drive side intact to ensure that the spacing remains identical – this is especially important with the rear hub, as uneven spacing can affect the chainline and the gear shifting.

3 Remove the axle from the drive side, clean the parts and check the cones for signs of wear, especially pitting. Be careful to collect all the bearings – sometimes these will need to be fished out with a suitable screwdriver. Set all the axle components to one side and clean the hub bearing surfaces.

4 If the freehub body needs replacing, you can remove it at this stage with a 10mm Allen key. The cassette body is usually factory fitted and tight, so you'll need a long Allen key. You may need to use a pipe for a little extra leverage to undo the bolt.

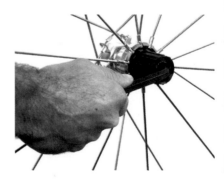

5 The bolt that retains the cassette body can be fully removed and the cassette body can be replaced if necessary. Be careful not to lose the washer that sits on the inside of the body. Set the torque wrench to 34.3-49Nm and re-tighten the bolt.

7 If you've disturbed or replaced the drive side cones, you'll have to accurately set and tighten the drive side before reassembling the hub. Once the axle is in place it's difficult to access the cones on the drive side as they're tucked into the freehub body.

6 Grease and reset the bearings into the hub as per front hubs. Nine 1/4in bearings are usually required, but double-check that you're returning the same amount as you removed. Reinsert the axle. The grease should be sufficient to hold the bearings in place, but do this over a bench in case they decide to escape.

8 Spin the non-drive side cone onto the axle and set the cone finger-tight. Add any spacers, washers and finally the lock nut. Finally set the cones. This is harder with the rear hub due to the inaccessible drive-side cones. It's therefore far easier to do this job with the wheel secured in an axle vice, and some mechanics even adjust the hub when it's back in the bike.

CAMPAGNOLO HUBS

FRONT HUB

1 Undo the axle end bolt with two 5mm Allen keys (see step 1 of rear hub servicing over the page) and remove the end – this is the part that retains the wheel in the forks and also allows the QR levers to fit through the hub.

2 Undo the retaining screw on the collar adjustment (this is either a cross-headed screw or a 3mm Allen screw).

3 Remove the adjustment collar, which threads to the outside of the axle – once this is removed, the axle is free, although the cone may still be held tight to the axle next to the bearings. A very gentle tap with a plastic mallet may be required to shift it.

4 Now pull the axle out. The bearings are held in plastic clips and under the white weather seals. The weather seals are very delicate, so it's best to leave them in place and work around them.

5 Strip out the bearings and replace if necessary. Flush out all the dirt and old grease with degreaser and make sure that the insides are clean and dried with a rag. Grease both sets of bearings before reassembling the axle with good-quality waterproof grease.

7 There's a split washer/spacer that centres the axle over the cone. Once this is in place, the threaded collar can be replaced and the cones set without any play – this is usually done to finger-tightness.

8 The fixed side of the hub has a dust cover that snaps into place over the axle and keeps the weather and muck out. Replace the QR and you're ready to ride. If the hub still has play in it when it's back in the forks, remove and retighten the adjustable collar.

6 Replace the axle with the cone collar on the fixed side. The adjustable side cone slips over the axle and rests on the bearings. Check the cone for pitting and replace the cone if necessary.

REAR HUB

1 Undo the end cap with two 5mm Allen keys – this will unscrew the axle end of the non-drive side. Remove the end cap on the non-drive side and the thin washer just behind it.

3 The collar may be tight, although it can usually be removed with your fingers. This also demonstrates how to adjust the play out of the hubs when rebuilding them, with a spanner on the adjustment collar and an Allen key in the end of the axle.

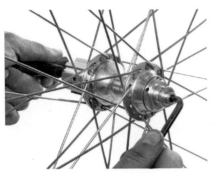

2 You can then undo and remove the adjusting collar from the axle. On this Record hub the retaining bolt requires a 3mm Allen key.

4 As with the front hub you'll now see a split washer and the weather seals, but unlike the front hub the axle won't be free just yet.

5 Turn the wheel around and use a 17mm cone spanner to undo the cassette-body locking collar. This is a left-hand thread (anti-clockwise) and the axle needs to be trapped at the same time with a 5mm Allen key in the fixed, drive-side axle end.

6 There's a direction arrow marked on the cassette-body locking collar. Remove the collar from the axle end. The cassette body will now easily pull away from the hub. Thoroughly clean and degrease the pawls and internals of the ratchet ring on the hub body. Rebuild using a very light grease.

7 The internals are as on a sealed bearing hub body, although Campagnolo pawls are retained in a circular spring clip, which prevents them from falling out when you pull the cassette body away. You can use an old toothbrush to get the freewheel mechanism really clean.

8 Check and grease the main axle bearings in both the drive and non-drive side of the hub shell – as with the front hub, don't attempt to remove the white weather seals.

9 The cone slides onto the axle, which can then be re-installed into the hub body. When the axle is pushed back into the hub, the cone collar will seat into the bearings. Turn the axle in the bearings and check for any notchy feeling, which may denote worn bearings or pitted cones.

11 Refit the split retaining washer and the adjusting collar (as on the front hub). Now adjust the bearings and nip up. Before replacing the cassette body, check the hub for play and re-adjust until the bearings feel silky smooth.

10 Turn the wheel over and reinstate the non-drive side cone collar – as with the front hub this simply slides over the axle and into place.

12 Once the axle is reinstated, and you're happy that the bearings are properly serviced, turn the wheel over and replace the cassette body – the pawls may require some fiddling to get into position, but the system is pretty simple. Replace the cassette-body locking collar (tightens anti-clockwise) and lastly the non-drive side axle end.

Tyres are a vital piece of equipment. It doesn't matter how good your steering, brakes and gears operate, ultimately it all depends on the tyres gripping the road. Perhaps because they have no moving parts, tyres are often neglected, but they're also uniquely vulnerable to damage from road debris. Fixing punctures is an inevitable part of being a cyclist.

REMOVING TYRES AND REPLACING A TUBE

1 Fix good rim tapes to the wheel. Use tapes that stick to the rim base, as they're less likely to move when you inflate the tyre. Make sure that there are no sharp objects in the rim and that all the spoke holes are covered.

3 Pull the tube away from the tyre and pack it away – you can fix it later. Check that there's nothing wrong with the rim tape beneath the tube, as it can sometimes come loose under the tyre and move, exposing a spoke hole that can pinch the tube. Double-check the tyre walls for thorns and anything that may have penetrated the tyre. Be careful not to get any debris in there either, as it may be sharp and cause another flat on inflation.

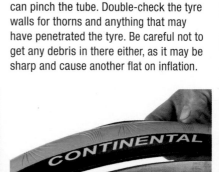

2 Most road tyres will come off easily with just one tyre lever. Push the tyre away to reveal the bead, slip the lever tip under the bead and simply pull the bead off. If you have to use two levers, pull one section off first and then move a little further around the rim. The second lever will be harder to pull, but should pop the tyre off easily. Run the lever around the rim, which will remove one side of the tyre from the rim. Don't remove the tyre completely at this point.

4 Slightly inflate the replacement tube with two strokes of a mini-pump, just enough for the tube to take shape but not so much that it becomes bigger than the diameter of the wheel. Next, insert the valve into the valve hole. Make sure that the valve is seated properly into the rim, then push the tyre over the top of the tube.

5 Work the tube carefully into the carcass of the tyre, away from the rim, inflating it slightly more if necessary. Beware of folds in the tube at this point and don't twist the tube as you return it to the tyre – this can pinch and even puncture once re-inflated, and may also mean that the tyre will inflate unevenly.

7 Pull the last part of the tyre onto the rim by hand, as a tyre lever can pinch the tube as you lever the tyre on. It can be a bit tricky with some tyres, so ask someone to help if possible. Once done, check that the bead hasn't snagged the tube or pinched it between the bead and the rim. This can push the tyre off the rim or make it roll unevenly, or even explode once the tyre has been pumped up to a decent pressure.

6 Now, start to return the open side of the tyre bead into the rim. Start at the valve hole and work the tyre either side with two hands, until there's only a small amount left.

8 Finally, pump the tyre up to the recommended pressure. If the tyre doesn't run true (it wobbles as you spin the wheel), re-seat it by letting most of the air out and pulling the tyre away from the bead. This will help the bead sit into the rim and usually "pops" the tyre into place.

REPAIRING AN INNER TUBE

1 Find the hole. This is usually a case of pumping up the tube and listening. A bucket of water is not required for this – just keep pumping until you can hear the hiss. Once you have the hole, place your finger and thumb over it, as you don't want to lose it.

2 Rough up the area around the hole with some sandpaper. This will help the glue penetrate the rubber and ensure the patch adheres properly. The glue is a contact adhesive (it works when the patch is placed on it), but needs to be applied to a grease-free and dry tube in order to work properly.

3 Apply plenty of glue to the area, starting at the hole and working outwards. Keep an eye on where the hole is so you can get the patch over it properly later on. Leave the glue for five minutes until it's almost completely dry.

4 Most fixable holes are covered by a 2cm patch. Apply firm pressure to the patch with your thumb, as you want the patch to be fully in place before you re-inflate. Stretch the tube gently by pulling either side of the patch – this will show if it has stuck. If it's a "pinch" flat or snakebite puncture, use two patches (one over each hole), rather than one big one.

5 Remove the plastic backing film from the centre. Don't pull it off from a corner, as it can pull the patch off with it. The backing is used to make sure you don't touch the underside of the patch, and so you can press it onto the tube easily.

7 Undo the small locking tip of the valve (Presta type only). Free it up by pressing it in a couple of times – this will enable the valve to pass air in easily, as it sometimes gets stuck after full inflation.

6 If you can dust the area with French chalk or talc, this will prevent the glue from sticking to the inside of the tyre carcass and help it slide into place as you inflate the tyre.

8 Push the pump head firmly onto the valve, with a thumb on the tyre to stop the valve vanishing into the hole. Engage the pump head's locking lever if it has one, and reinflate the tyre to the recommended pressure.

TUBULAR TYRES

Tubular tyres combine the inner tube and casing into a single, lightweight unit that's glued onto a hook less "sprint" rim. Contrary to popular belief, tubulars are actually quite easy to install – it can be a bit messy the first few times you attempt it, but in time you get better at the job.

1 Deflate the old tyre and remove it by pushing it off and ripping it from the old glue. Cleaning the rim is essential – new aluminium rims can have oil and manufacturing cutting compounds still on the surface of the rim, preventing the glue from sticking.

2 Used rims will have hard lumps of glue, and where these have collected there's a chance that they will push the tyre out of shape. Brake debris and road dirt can also prevent the tyre from sticking, so clean the whole wheel and allow time for it to dry off completely before you start to apply glue.

3 Use a wire brush on really stubborn old glue, and clean all the dust and debris away before you start to apply new glue. Be careful with carbon rims not to scratch the braking surface of the rim. Carbon rims need careful treatment – be sure to check with the manufacturer as to their recommended choice of solvent and cleaning procedure.

4 Most glues for tubulars are contact adhesives. These glues work when they are dry or nearly dry (tacky) and once they have hardened they are extremely resilient, especially to shearing forces. My favourite glues are Continental, Vittoria and Tubasti – Continental is the most readily available and is very consistent and dries in next to no time.

5 Apply a layer of glue to the rim. You can use your finger, but this is messy stuff. I find the best way is with a 1/2in paintbrush. Apply another coat of glue when the previous one has dried. Don't rush, but be careful to get the rim covered quickly. Keep the glue well away from the spoke holes and try not to pool glue in places, as it drips easily.

7 Then apply a final coat of glue to the tyre only, not the rim. Wait 10-20 minutes before starting to attach it. The glue should be almost dry again, but just a little tacky – make sure that there are no wet areas, especially on the tyre, as you are about to handle the glued part. Deflate the tyre once it's nearly dry and you're ready to install it.

6 Brush a coat of glue onto the underside of the tyre. I usually do this with the tyre partially inflated and take care to spread the glue very evenly. On many tyres the first coat will be absorbed into the cloth of the base tape, so two coats of glue will be needed. Leave the tyre and rim for at least an hour to allow the glue to cure.

8 With the wheel standing upright on a hard floor, insert the valve stem into the rim and seat the tyre on either side of the hole. Press firmly so that the tyre seats into the rim. Pull down with your hands to both sides, away from the stem, working around the rim, pressing and pushing very firmly, until reaching the bottom with only a short section of tyre not yet in place. ▶

9 Lift the wheel and use your thumbs to push the remaining section onto the rim. To get the last section of tyre onto the rim without making a mess, grab the remaining four or five inches of tub and lift it away from, and over, the rim. If you struggle with this, flip the wheel over and hold the wheel at the valve hole onto the floor with your toes (take your shoes off for this!). You can then pull with your fingers rather than push with your thumbs.

10 Inflate the tyre enough for it to take some shape, and start to bed the tyre into the rim. Positioning the tyre can take a bit of patience, as there needs to be equal amounts of backing tape overlapping the edge of the rim. Flip the wheel several times to make sure that it is symmetrical.

11 The valve should be vertical in the rim hole and not angled, which makes it very hard to inflate and will also mean there is a high spot to the tyre where it is not seated correctly into the rim.

12 Spin the wheel to check for wobbles in the tyre tread and readjust until the tyre runs as true as possible before the glue starts to set. Once you're happy that the glue is covered and the tyre is central to the rim, pump the tyres up to maximum pressure and leave for a minimum of 12 hours before you ride them.

When shift levers migrated northwards from the frame to the handlebars courtesy of Shimano's STI integrated shifter/brake levers, it made road bikes much more user friendly but also more complicated. Other manufacturers have their own options now, but the fundamentals of indexed derailleur gear systems are common to all.

REAR DERAILLEUR

ADJUSTMENT AND SETUP

1 The rear mech needs to be installed onto the gear hanger. Check that the hanger is straight and that the threads are clean and uncrossed. If the hanger is bent or the mech cage is twisted, the system won't work. Use some grease or Ti-Prep lube on the threads to prevent the bolt from seizing.

2 The inner wire is clamped onto the rear mech by a washer. To see how this works, look for a channel moulded onto the body of the mech – the washer will be marked where the cable has been. Screw the gear barrel adjuster fully in and put the

shifter in the highest gear before pulling the cable tight and clamping it with the bolt.

3 Adjust the limit screw marked "H" when the chain is in the smallest sprocket (highest gear). It's important that the chain can run smoothly over the sprocket and can't move any further down the block, trapping the chain between frame and cassette. It's a good idea to fit the chain now.

4 Next, adjust the limit screw marked "L" when the gear is in the largest sprocket. Double-check that the chain can reach this sprocket, and also that the chain can't jump over the top of the cassette and into the wheel. Also check that the mech can't hit the spokes of the wheel.

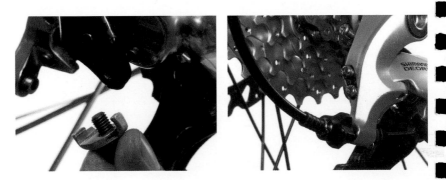

5 Place the bike in a workstand, leaving your hands free to pedal the bike and adjust the cable tension. Run through each gear. If it struggles to make the next sprocket, the cable is too loose, so you'll need to tighten the cable by screwing the barrel adjuster anti-clockwise. Now change back through the gears (large to small cog) and check if there's a delay in the shift or if the chain stays stuck in one gear – if so, the cable is too tight and you'll need to loosen it by turning the adjuster clockwise.

6 If you can't get the derailleur to shift cleanly in both directions, check the cable and housing for fraying or drag and replace if necessary. Make sure the parallelogram mechanism is running smoothly by lubricating with a light Teflon-based lube, especially the pivot points and internal springs.

7 Rear mechs work best with free-running jockey wheels. These can be replaced when the plastic wheels wear out. This improves shifting and helps keep the chain in contact with the sprockets on the cassette. To replace the jockey wheels, remove the pivot screws, paying attention to how they go back together.

8 Strip and rebuild the jockey wheels after long periods of wet weather. The top jockey wheel may have a sealed bearing in it. It's worth stripping and reassembling both wheels. Clean them completely and reassemble using a Teflon lubricant. Make sure that the jockey wheel is replaced so that it rotates in the right direction.

FRONT DERAILLEUR

ADJUSTMENT AND SETUP

1 Angle the mech so that it's exactly parallel with the big chainring. If you can't get the mech into this position, you may have problems with the chainline and, if so, you may need a different length bottom bracket.

2 If the angle is slightly out, the shifting will be sloppy, so make sure you set the angle carefully. If it's angled too far outwards, it'll foul the crank when the pedals are turned. A good chainline is imperative, so make sure that the chain can

access all of the rear sprockets when in the inner chainring. You can also see here that the ideal mech position is parallel with the outer (big) chainring.

3 The distance between the outside mech plate and the teeth of the chainring should be no more than 2–3mm. This will ensure that the mech is correctly positioned to cope with the difference in size of the inner and big rings.

4 This set-up is with smaller chainrings (Compact drive), and although it'll probably work OK, the gap at the bottom of the cage is much greater than at the top, the result being a sloppy shift. If you're using Compact cranks, consider a Compact-specific front mech.

5 This SRAM front mech is positioned perfectly for tight and crisp changes – check that the outside plate clears all the teeth, though 3mm will allow for the chain pick-up and will happily clear the teeth of the chainrings.

6 Next, attach the gear cable. Make sure that the gear-shifter is in its lowest position so that the cable is at its slackest and the front mech is over the inner ring. Pull the cable through the clamp firmly. Trap the cable in the clamp and check that it's in the right place, as this can affect the shift. Now, adjust the low-limit stop screw.

7 Adjust the limit screw marked "L" first. Place the rear mech in the biggest sprocket and the front onto the smallest, as this is the furthest the chain will travel. Then set the front mech so it only just clears the inside of the plate without rubbing.

8 Now, adjust the limit screw marked "H". Put the chain onto the big chainring (this may over-shift at first) and work the rear mech through all the gears. You'll notice that the chain changes angle considerably, but it'll cope with most of the gears on this chainring. Set the limit screw so that it just clears the chain in the smallest rear sprocket.

REPLACING GEAR CABLES

Cable replacement varies depending on which shift levers you have. Modern shifters are all integrated into the brake levers, but the three main manufacturers route the cables in slightly different ways. Older Shimano units have exposed gear cable housing from the tops of the hoods – the current generation has the cables under the bar tape except for the cheapest models. SRAM and Campagnolo have always used concealed cables.

1 To thread the cable through the lever mechanism, place the gear-shifter in the highest gear position. All systems require the lever and mech to be in top gear, so that the cable is slack and the nipple can be pushed out of the lever.

2 On Shimano and SRAM levers, you'll be able to see the white plastic cable-carrier. In this position the cable can be pushed through easily.

3 On Shimano levers, the cable simply passes straight through the lever and out of the cable port on the other side.

4 SRAM shifter cables are inserted at the inside, near the bottom of the lever housing, and exit the lever at the top.

5 On SRAM levers, as with Campagnolo, the outer cable can be taped and fitted into the handlebar before the tape is applied.

6 New Campagnolo cables have a sharp, pointed end that makes threading the cable through the lever very easy.

7 Pull the cable through until the nipple seats itself in the cable-carrier.

DOWN-TUBE SHIFTERS

Down-tube shifters were once the only gear-shifting choice. Nowadays they're rarely used – some climbers swap the front-mech shifter for a down-tube lever to save a few ounces, but the weight saved isn't really worth the effort. Down-tube levers mean that you have to take your hands off the handlebars to shift, but there's less cable and friction in the system, so they do last and provide very crisp shifts. Gear-adjusters are attached to most older frames designed for use with down-tube shifters. The gear-adjusters attach via a boss that is brazed to the frame. Campagnolo gear-adjusters rely on knurled-threaded adjusters with a spring under them to hold them in place – these do require cleaning and lubricating with a light oil to keep them easy to adjust. Shimano adjusters have a lever that can be turned to micro-adjust the gears as you ride. Seeing as most frames come without the standard-type bosses, these adjusters are becoming rare.

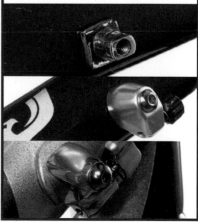

ELECTRONIC GROUPSETS

CAMPAGNOLO EPS AND SHIMANO DI2

Shimano's Di2 Electronic shifting groupset has been in action for a few seasons now and is slowly becoming more popular for consumers. All the set-up principles for frames are the same as cable gears, the only difference is the cable set up, and it needs a battery. Adjustment is done electronically too, so although it may seem a bit space age and Formula 1, electronic gears are actually easier to maintain than their cabled counterparts.

1 Frames built specifically for electronic shifting have the cables routed inside the frame tubes, emerging from the frame near to the derailleurs. If you want to retrofit electronic shifting to a traditional frame, you'll have to cable tie the wires to the frame.

2 Gear limit adjustment is exactly the same as for mechanical systems, with high and low stop screws on the mech. This Shimano Di2 derailleur has Allen key screws accessed from the rear.

3 Indexing adjustment is done automatically when you press the adjustment button. On Shimano systems the button is located on this unit attached to the brake cables under the stem. Campagnolo's system has a button on the shift lever itself.

4 Front shifting is where electronic systems make the most difference, as the throw required to move the chain between chainrings is much greater than between sprockets. Positioning and setup is identical to cable systems.

Even the fittest, strongest cyclist can put out less power than a small lawnmower, so there's not much scope for wasting any effort. The power put in at the pedals reaches the road via the cranks, bottom bracket, chain and rear sprockets, and the difference between a worn, dirty and unloved drivetrain and a clean, smooth, silent one is significant.

CASSETTE SERVICE AND REPLACEMENT

REMOVAL

1 Cassette servicing is best done with the wheel intact and the tyres still attached to the rim (in case you have to rest the wheel on the floor or lean on it for extra purchase).

2 The cassette lock-ring tool fits into the serrated inside of the lock-ring. Shimano and Campagnolo use the same principle, but not the same tool!

3 The standard socket-type tool can be held in place with the QR skewer to prevent it from rounding off the cassette lock-ring or slipping and causing injury or damage.

4 This double-sided tool also features a central locating pin (it's a personal favourite of mine!). It means you can use it with either system, and the pin helps hold the tool in place and allows for a firmer grip.

5 Remove the cassette using a chain whip and cassette lock-ring removal tool. The chain whip prevents the cassette from turning (freewheeling), and should be positioned so that the chain on the tool can wrap around the sprocket enough to prevent it from spinning when you push on the wrench.

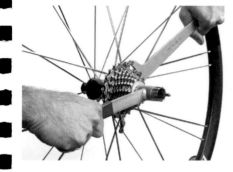

6 Campagnolo 10-speed requires a chain whip with a 10-speed chain end to prevent damage to the sprockets and slipping as you apply pressure.

7 Shimano systems can use a standard chain whip. Stand over the wheel with the cassette facing away from you. Hold the chain whip in your left hand and the lock-ring tool in your right. Set the whip over the second-biggest gear and position the tools as shown. Pushing down with both hands will undo the lock-ring.

8 The first two or three cassette sprockets will be loose, so be careful not to drop them. Lay the wheel flat on the workbench and take the sprockets off one by one, placing them down in the order in which they came off the wheel.

REFITTING

1 Apply a thin layer of grease or anti-seize to the cassette body before you slide the cassette back into place. This will prevent the cassette body from rusting. If there's any corrosion on the body, use a brass suede-shoe brush to clean it off.

2 Shimano cassettes sometimes require a spacer behind the cassette. If there's one there when you take the cassette off, remember to put it back, especially when they're not Shimano. Bear this in mind if you're setting up the gears too, as it can change the spacing and therefore the indexing for the rear mech.

3 Better-quality cassettes have the first few (four on Shimano, two on Campagnolo) large cassette sprockets attached to a "spider" or aluminium carrier to save some weight without losing rigidity.

4 On Campagnolo cassettes, the second pair of sprockets are also held on a carrier – in Record, these first two clusters are made from titanium. There's a spacer that must be replaced between the first and second pairs.

5 The remaining cassette sprockets are loose and have a spacer (marked nine- or 10-speed) to ensure the correct spacing and alignment of the sprockets. Campagnolo cassettes require another wider spacer before the loose sprockets go on.

7 Refit the lock-ring. It has serrations on the underside that engage with similar serrations on the top sprocket to prevent it from vibrating loose.

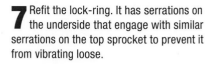

6 The final one or two sprockets may not require the spacers, as they're machined with integral spacers. If you've got everything right, all the sprockets should be evenly spaced.

8 Once the cassette is in place, tighten the lock-ring to 35–50Nm. You'll be surprised how tight this is, but the cassette bears a considerable load and needs to be checked for tightness regularly.

CHECKING THE CHAIN FOR WEAR

1 Measure across 24 links of the chain – it should measure 12in. If it's more than that, the chain has stretched beyond a usable length. A chain in this state will start to wear other components and shifting will become increasingly erratic. You can also use one of the various chain-measuring tools on the market.

FITTING SHIMANO CHAINS

1 This darker-coloured, flat-ended pin marks the spot where the chain was first joined. If you're removing the chain to clean it and have a new link to rejoin the chain, find this link and break the chain exactly opposite it.

2 For a very quick visual check, put the chain on the biggest chainring and smallest cassette sprocket. If you can pull the chain off the chainring and it can clear the tip of one of the chainring teeth, or the chain moves excessively at the top and bottom of the chainring, this means the chain may need to be replaced.

2 Remove the old chain and measure the new one next to it. Depending on the type of chain, you'll have to remove a certain number of links from one end. Leave the "open" plates or external link end and remove links from the other end, leaving internal links ready for rejoining. This keeps the factory fitted end complete.

3 Thread the new chain through the rear mech jockey wheels and over the chainwheel. Don't put it back on the chainring until you've joined the chain, as the slack will make it easier to rejoin the two ends. The Shimano chain is joined with this special pin to make sure that the link is pushed in the correct way. Grease the pin so that it'll go in easily.

4 Push the link through using a quality Shimano chain-compatible chain-rivet tool. This Park tool has shaped jaws to prevent the side plates squeezing together. Keep the chain straight and turn the handle firmly and slowly to make sure that the pin goes through totally straight.

5 The Park chain tool is set up so that it stops once the link is in place (there's a circlip on the threaded shaft that prevents you going too far). There's a definite click as the pin passes through the link. When you reach this point, back off the handle and check that the pin is in place.

6 Although Shimano 10-speed chains use the same principles as a nine-speed chain, they're noticeably narrower and they use a specific 10-speed pin (rivet).

▶ **7** For 10-speed chains make sure that you use a genuine HG tool and that the pin is always pushed through from the outside. Check that the pin protrudes an equal distance either side of the plates.

9 Once the pin is in place there may be a little stiffness in the link, which may jump as you pedal the gears backwards. To remove a stiff link, first add some lube to it and push it into an inverted V-shape.

8 When the Shimano (nine- or 10-speed) pin is through to the other side and the fatter part of the pin is equally spaced on either side of the link plates, snap off the guide with some pliers. Obviously, you need to do this before you check the gears are working.

10 Then place your thumbs on the links to either side of this link. Grip the chain and very gently push the chain against itself. This very careful twisting should free the link immediately.

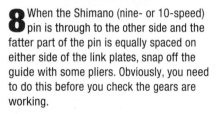

SRAM CHAINS

1 To get the correct chain length, measure the chain so that it's tight when placed from biggest sprocket to biggest chainring, bypassing the rear mech (it's easiest to do this before the rear mech is attached).

3 Then install the rear mech and thread the chain through the jockey wheels over the chainrings and through the front mech, join the two open ends of chain with the Power Link and slot the pins into place – they'll sit halfway, not quite bedded into the closed position.

2 Then add two links to this length. SRAM chains are joined with a special Power Link, which joins the chain between two rollers – you'll need to remove the side plates from both ends of the chain so they join the chain between two rollers.

4 Brace the rear wheel and push the crank arm to snap the Power Link fully closed. 10-speed Power Links aren't reusable – next time you break the chain, do so opposite the link and use a new one to rejoin it – it'll seat into place, and the main advantage is that no tools are required and it's impossible to get a stiff link.

CAMPAGNOLO CHAINS

1 The 10-speed Campagnolo chain has a serial number stamped on the external link. This is very important, as it denotes the link that needs to be left untampered with. The external links are designed specifically to face a certain way to accept the countersunk pin that joins the two ends of chain together.

2 A Campagnolo 10-speed HD chain-pin has a detachable guide pin and a hollow rivet – this guide pin simply slots into the rivet and can be taken out once the chain has been joined.

3 The HD pin is always placed on the inside of the drivetrain, so as to be pushed outwards of the bike (for the reason explained in step 1).

4 Measure the chain in the small sprocket and inner chain wheel. When the chain ends are pulled together you're looking for a gap of around 15mm between the chainline along the bottom and the top of the lower jockey wheel.

5 The rear mech should just take up the slack in the chain, and the chain should run clear of the jockey wheel cage guides (the tab at the rear of this cage).

6 Place the chain on the big ring and link up the chain with the connecting pin. Join the chain under the chainring from the inside out – double-check that you have the stamped external plate on the outside before you do this.

8 It may appear over-complicated, but special "HD Link" rejoining links are required if the chain is broken and needs to be rejoined. Measure the same length of links and remove the same amount from the chain opposite the first join. This can then be installed with two HD pins.

7 The Campagnolo chain tool has a locking pin that pushes across the internal and external links to ensure that the chain is held tightly and the links are perfectly aligned.

SHIMANO HTII AND SRAM GXP CRANKS

1 Shimano, SRAM and Campagnolo all use very similar outboard bearing bottom bracket cups – they use the same pattern spanner to fit, but the bearings aren't interchangeable.

2 Both Shimano and SRAM systems have the axle permanently attached to the drive side and passing through the two cups. Apply a little grease to the parts that come into contact with the bearings.

3 Simply slide the axle through the cups and push the crank against the bearing on the drive side. It's quite a snug fit and may need a gentle tap with a rubber mallet to seat properly.

4 SRAM GXP cranks have an ISIS-style splined fitting on the end of the axle. This will protrude from the cups to allow the left-hand crank to tighten onto, and secure, the system in one action.

5 There's an aluminium sleeve on the inside of the left-hand crank, inside the carbon arm, which requires a little grease on the inside to prevent it from seizing.

7 Shimano HTII cranks have a finer splined interface on the left side. Put a little grease on the splines and push the crank arm on, being sure to orientate it correctly.

6 There's a simple captive bolt on the left-hand crank, which tightens the whole system and also removes the crank in one, so as you undo the bolt the cranks will pull off the end of the axle.

8 Fit the plastic end cap and use Shimano's TL-FC16 tool (or equivalent) to tighten it. This cap preloads the bearings, so don't overtighten it. Then tighten the two opposing pinch bolts to secure the crank.

CAMPAGNOLO ULTRA-TORQUE

1 The BB cups install into the frame in the same way as Shimano's and using the same pattern spanner. Tighten the cups to 35Nm. Use a little light grease on the insides of the cups where the bearings will sit.

2 The drive-side crank is inserted first. The bearing is factory fitted to the inside of the cranks and can be replaced if necessary.

3 Push the crank into the BB cups so that the bearing fits flush with the edge of the cups.

4 Once the drive-side bearing is in place, you can fit the spring clip. This prevents the drive side from falling out when you insert the left-hand crank. Wiggle the cranks to make sure that the spring clip has retained the bearing properly.

5 Line up the left-hand crank with the drive-side crank – it's possible to fit the cranks "wonky", as the serrated mating point is symmetrical. There's also a washer (already inside the BB cup in this picture) that needs to fit over the BB axle.

6 As with the drive side, the left-hand crank-side bearing fits flush with the BB cup and is sealed with a rubber seal.

7 Once lined up, it should be very easy to push the two crank sides together – the axle will mesh perfectly inside the BB shell.

8 Apply some grease to the thread of the bolt and, with a socket-set extension bar, pass the bolt into the hole on the drive side of the assembly, then locate the thread in the centre of the axle. Use a torque wrench to tighten the bolt to 42Nm.

SQUARE TAPER, ISIS AND OCTALINK CRANKS

While most bikes now come with two-piece cranks and outboard bottom bracket bearings (Shimano HTII, Campagnolo Ultra-Torque etc), older ones may still have traditional inboard bottom brackets with crank arms fitted to either side. While square taper, ISIS and Octalink cranks have different axle interface patterns, the principles of assembly are the same for each.

1 On standard cranks, the fixing bolt has an 8mm Allen head with the washer as an integral part of the bolt. Old-style cranks still use a 14mm or 15mm hex-headed bolt and washer that can be protected by a separate dust cap.

2 The bolt has a washer/cover around it to protect the threads inside the crank. There may also be a washer (usually on Campagnolo only) behind the bolt, so make sure that you remove this also.

3 Once you've removed the bolts and washers, remove the crank using a crank-puller. This tool is essential for taking the cranks off the bike, and good ones won't damage the threads or the end of the axle. Clean out any dirt from the crank threads with a squirt of spray-lube.

4 The crank-puller has a central bolt, and once it's threaded into the crank as far as it'll go, the central bolt can be tightened to "push" the crank away from the BB axle. Undo the centre bolt first so it fits as flush as possible, being careful to get it in straight.

5 The easiest puller to use is one with an arm attached to the end of the centre bolt – they are useful for travelling toolkits when you might not have room for a big spanner. However, it's worth noting that most pullers accept a 15mm spanner, so you can use a pedal-spanner to tighten the removing bolt.

7 Once you've correctly inserted the puller, tighten the arm (or central bolt) towards the BB axle. The arm rests on the end of the axle and the pushing/pulling motion forces the crank off the square-axle taper. The crank will try to drop off onto the floor, so be careful to keep hold of it.

6 ISIS and Octalink cranks have a hollow round axle and therefore require a larger head on the crank-puller – Park's remover can accept either types and is supplied with a pair of different-sized adaptors. ISIS axles have a symmetrical splined pattern on the axle, and it's worth cleaning this every time you remove the crank arms. Shimano Octalink cranks are very different, so don't try to mix them up.

8 Some cranks have "captive" bolts. These have a puller built in, and the crank bolt is held captive so that the undoing action of the crank bolt also removes the crank for you. These are recommended on ISIS and Octalink, and are also fitted to some Shimano cranksets.

FITTING STANDARD BOTTOM BRACKETS

1 Thread and BB preparation is essential. The tools needed to do this job are very expensive and require careful handling. This may mean you have to get a good bike shop to do the first few (cutting) tasks for you, but it's essential that the threads are cleaned and the faces squared up before you start.

2 The threads need to be thoroughly cleaned (use an old toothbrush and a strong degreaser). Remove any oxide build-up and then dry off completely. Dress the threads with a good-quality grease – waterproof greases are best – and use

copper slip on titanium components. Some mechanics will use thread-lock on Italian BBs to prevent the cups from loosening, but be careful as this can create long-term problems.

3 The new unit will have one removable side, which is usually on the non-drive side. Pull this off, so that the unit can be installed into the drive side first. This side has a left-hand thread and tightens anti-clockwise.

4 The non-drive-side cup is right-hand threaded and is designed to be flange-less, so it can accommodate a variety of widths of BB. This tightens clockwise and will mesh with the cartridge inside the shell. Most Shimano brackets have a taper on the inside that allows it to self-locate. Again, tighten this with your fingers until there's

about 1cm (1/2in) of thread left showing. If the threads have been properly prepared, you'll be able to turn the unit into place with your fingers.

5 Shimano brackets use a special tool that sits in serrations around the edge of the cup. Some brackets use a set of holes that accept a pin spanner or peg tool and a lock-ring to hold it in position. If you don't get the right tools for the bracket, you risk making a mess of the unit and your frame.

6 Campagnolo BBs have a smaller ring of serrations and use the same remover as their cassettes. Be careful with poorly fitting or worn tools, as these can easily be rounded out if you don't take care.

7 The best tool to remove Campagnolo BBs is one that can be threaded into the ends of the BB axle and held captive. These are much safer and easier when exerting plenty of pressure to remove stubborn units. Holding everything firmly in position like this leaves you free to get on with the job.

8 Next, use the BB tool to tighten the unit into the frame. Make sure that the shoulder of the unit on the drive side is tight up against the frame first. This is to make sure that the chainset will sit in the right place to achieve the most efficient chainline. Then snug down the non-drive-side and tighten both cups to 40–50Nm (check manufacturer's recommendation).

FITTING CHAINRINGS

Fitting chainrings is very simple, but make sure that you get the correct size for your crank. There are a number of standards for the PCD (Pitch Circle Diameter) of the mounting bolts – Campagnolo use 135mm, Shimano uses 130mm for standard rings or 110mm for compact rings, and so on.

1 All chainrings will have an alignment arrow, which usually lines the chainrings up with the crank. Another giveaway to orientation on the outer (big) chainwheel is a chain pip – an aluminium grommet that stops the chain getting jammed between the spider and the crank, should the chain unship.

2 The inner chainwheel may also have an orientation mark (especially if it's on a triple crank, and the ring has grooves and ramps for the chain to shift along). Usually, the graphics on the outside of both chainrings will have been designed to line up. Once the rings are aligned correctly, hold them together with the first bolt as they're unlikely to be able to stay in place.

3 On Campagnolo Record cranks, one of the bolts threads directly into the crank arm. There's a spacer and a shim to provide exact alignment, so be careful to reinstall these when reassembling them, and place this bolt in first.

4 Use a decent-quality grease or copper slip on the bolts and directly into the bolt-holes. Not only does this prevent the bolts from seizing, it also stops them "drying out" and creaking as time goes by.

6 Torx key fittings are now being used on new Campagnolo cranks, so be sure to use the right tools and carry them with you in your toolkit.

5 Most chainring bolts take a 5mm Allen key and need to be tightened to 6Nm (aluminium) or 10Nm (steel). Chainring bolts should be tightened gradually and in sequence (that is, not from left to right but from opposite bolt to opposite bolt).

7 Chainring bolts can rotate in the crank, so use a bolt-wrench to hold the nut at the back and prevent it from spinning.

FIXED WHEELS

Fixed wheel bikes, with a single fixed sprocket that doesn't freewheel, are used for track racing on the velodrome and for winter training out on the roads. The fixed wheel is the simplest and most robust bicycle drivetrain there is, so it makes sense for use in poor conditions.

1 Fixed-wheel bikes use front and rear hubs with nuts rather than a QR skewer. Threaded nuts will hold the chain tension far longer than a QR skewer, which can slip. QR skewers are also not allowed on track race bikes.

2 Track bikes have rear-facing dropouts and 120mm-spaced hubs (rather than 130mm of a road bike). Rear-facing dropouts offer a stronger and simpler solution to adjusting chain tension and accommodating variations in sprocket (gear) sizes.

3 On fixed, always use a 1/8in chain (they're wider than a 3/32in mech one), and if you use a single chainring, check the chain tension regularly. Beefier track chains stay put if the chain wobbles a bit over bumps or when pedalling fast. 1/8in chains are practically indestructible.

4 This chain fastens with a screw and a nut on the other side – it isn't a problem that they stick out, as the chain doesn't pass through mechs. This makes it easier to remove and change chains, and it's handy for cleaning too.

5 Chainline and tension are all-important. A track single chain-wheel, mounted to a specific crank (Miche, TA, Shimano, Campagnolo, etc) and suitably matched BB is the best option to get the chainline accurate. To get the chainline spot on, it's best to get a specific track crank and matching BB, like this Campagnolo set-up.

7 To remove the wheel, slacken the wheel nuts fully and slide the wheel forwards in the dropouts. This will allow you to remove the chain from the chainring and the sprocket. Remove the chain from the sprocket and wrap around the seat stay as shown here – this will allow the wheel to be slid out backwards.

6 You must line up the chain so that the sprocket is directly behind the chainring, especially if you're riding fixed, as the chain may unship if the chainline is wrong. To adjust the chainline, you may have to change the BB axle or fit an adjustable BB that can be moved from side to side slightly.

8 When returning the wheel to the bike, the chain can be wrapped over the chainring and sprocket. This will mean that the chain is too slack and you'll have to re-tension the drive. If the chain is sagging at the top and bottom, like this, it's way too loose to ride on.

9 To tension the chain, pull the track nuts back in the dropouts with the chain on the sprocket and chainwheel. Then tighten the nuts up finger tight.

10 You can then use the 15mm track nut wrench. Pull firmly backwards on the wheel (this is best done in a work-stand or with someone to help) and nip up the track nuts on both sides of the bike.

11 You may have to centralise the rear wheel and fully tighten the drive side first. Make sure that the wheel is central at the seat stays and chainstays just behind the bottom bracket before fully tightening the non-drive side. Hold the wheel firmly in position as you re-tighten the wheel nuts.

12 The correct chain tension will allow the wheel to rotate easily, and this means running with a little slack in the chain. Loosening the nuts slightly and slapping the chain with your nut wrench will slacken the chain a little if it's too tight.

07

Mountain bike-style disc brakes are just starting to appear on road bikes, but the vast majority of bikes are equipped with cable-activated rim brakes. The venerable calliper brake has undergone a lot of development over the years, with the latest generation of dual-pivot brakes delivering ample power and control. Efficient brakes are essential for safe, fast riding, so you need to keep on top of maintenance.

RELEASING BRAKES

All road brakes have a facility that allows you to back off the brakes in order to remove the wheels – the loosening of the brake calliper allows the tyre to pass easily through the brake pads

1 On Campagnolo brakes, the small aluminium button on the inside of the brake lever needs to be depressed before the wheels can be removed.

2 Once released, this will let the levers swing out further from the bar, releasing the pads away from the wheel rim. The release button should pop back into place when you pull the brake lever – check before riding.

3 On Shimano brakes, the QR lever is a cam on the cable clamp that moves the anchor point of the cable to allow the callipers to open. Turn the lever to point upwards to open.

4 Make sure the lever points back down in the closed position before riding.

FITTING BRAKE CALLIPERS

1 Rear brake callipers have a shorter fixing bolt and nut than front brakes. The brake bridge is drilled to take the recessed bolt shown here.

3 Brake callipers attach to the frame and fork with Allen key nuts. They have a variety of lengths to fit different fork crowns. Fatter fork crowns and wider brake bridges need longer fixing nuts. Brakes have to have at least 1cm of thread held by the nut for safety's sake.

2 Fit a star washer in between the brake and the frame to secure the calliper and prevent the brake from loosening under normal conditions.

4 Install the wheels and tighten the calliper fixing bolts while squeezing the pads onto the rim. This will roughly centre the brake over the rims and allow you to install the cables and adjust the brake pads. ▶

5 Centring the brakes makes the most of the braking efficiency and prevents the pads from rubbing on the rim. The brakes will also respond faster and feel better at the lever when accurately centred.

7 Campagnolo calliper springs can be adjusted for tension too, which just allows for fine tuning the feel at the lever for personal preference rather than improving brake function.

6 Shimano brakes can be centred without disturbing the brake fixing bolt. The adjustment screw on the top of the brake allows for fine tuning and perfect alignment.

8 SRAM callipers use a smaller 10mm spanner to centre the brake pads over the rim – when using a spanner like this always double-check that the fixing bolt is still tight in the frame/fork after adjusting.

BRAKE PAD ALIGNMENT

1 Brake pads are secured to the calliper arms with a single bolt each side, either an Allen key type or (as on the Campagnolo brakes shown) a Torx head bolt.

2 Simply loosen the bolt, align the pad to the rim – ensuring that it doesn't rub on the tyres or come off the bottom of the rim – and retighten.

3 As the pads wear, they'll start to strike the rim nearer and nearer the tyre. Check them regularly and readjust when necessary.

4 Campagnolo brake pads include a domed washer, letting you adjust the angle of the face of the pad relative to the rim. A small amount of toe-in (the front of the pads hitting the rim first) can prevent brake squeal.

FITTING CARTRIDGE BRAKE PADS

Many brake pads are the cartridge type, with replaceable pads slid into a shoe that can remain attached to the brake, minimising the need for readjustment.

1 Campagnolo pads simply slide into place. Push the old pads out of the slots and apply a very small amount of light grease or Vaseline to the slots in the shoe.

2 The pads are left and right-handed – make sure you put them in the correct sides. They're a tight fit and may require a fair bit of force to push into place. The open end of the cartridge should always face back so that the rotation of the wheel pushes them in, not out.

3 Shimano pads are a less tight fit, but have a screw that retains the pad in the cartridge.

4 They will slide in and out very easily once this screw is loosened.

CANTILEVER BRAKES

Cantilever brakes, pivoting on bosses welded to the frame and fork, are the standard option for cyclo cross and touring bikes. Their main benefit is a lot of clearance around the brake, for mud (in the case of 'cross) or big tyres and mudguards (in the case of tourers).

1 To remove the wheel, you have to unhook the straddle-wires, squeeze the pads together and unhook the straddle cable end.

2 Once the cable is unhooked, both sides of the brake fall away and will allow any tyre to be removed easily – this would be impossible with a standard calliper brake.

3 Replacing the standard fixed-length straddle wires with an older-style yoke and separate straddle will let you set the straddle further away from the tyres and adjust the feel of the brake. They also allow the brakes to be fully released when removing wheels quickly.

4 The principles of pad alignment are the same as for calliper brakes, but remember that as cantilever pads wear they strike the rim lower down (rather than higher up, as with callipers). Centre cantilever brakes using the Allen key spring tension adjusters on each brake arm.

CABLE REPLACEMENT

Damaged cables and water inside the cable outers will slow your braking down considerably. A damaged, kinked or frayed inner wire will give a sloppy or stiff lever action. Replacing the cable run is the best way to solve this, but stripping out the inner and using a quality spray lube can be a short-term fix. A notchy brake feel can result from added friction – the inner cable rubbing on either a burr at the end of the outer cable or a damaged frame cable stop. It's rare for cables to snap, but they can fray at the clamp bolts, which can make future adjustment difficult.

1 All systems require the cable outer to enter the rear of the brake lever. Make sure that the cable has been neatly cut and there are no sharp edges on the inside.

2 Shimano STI lever housings bury the cable nipple retainer deep inside the lever housing. Flick the lever to one side to allow the lever to fall further forwards and allow easy access.

3 Once the inner cable is in place the grommet can be returned to its position in the lever housing.

4 Campagnolo cables feature a sharp uncut end that makes it very easy to thread the inner wire through the lever.

5 SRAM brake cabling is very similar to Campagnolo's (although it is slightly easier to install).

6 Greasing the brake cable nipple will prevent friction and stop any noises developing as the levers are applied, and it prevents wear and tear on the cable around the nipple too.

7 Cables should be measured (it's easiest to use the old cables as a template) and cut using a quality cable cutter. Make sure that the ends of the cable are flat – they can be tidied up with a metal file – and that the inner nylon part is open at the ends.

8 Unlike gear cables, it is only necessary to add a ferrule where the cable will contact the frame stops. The V-brake noodle has its own built-in ferrule. New brake cables usually have a factory fitted ferrule on one end – I always start with this one at the lever adjuster.

9 The rear brake cable must be precision-cut so that the curve of the cable is unhindered and smooth. Overlong cables flap about and create friction. However, short cables will pull on the callipers and potentially de-centralise them over the rims.

11 Thread the inner cable through the fixing bolt and pull the callipers together onto the rim. Fasten the inner cable into the calliper using a 5mm Allen key. Leave 20–30mm of cable to allow for further adjustment, and cut the cable with a sharp cable cutter.

10 Cable doughnuts are used to prevent the cable slapping on the top tube and wearing out the paintwork (the noise of flapping cables is also highly annoying).

12 Lastly, add a cable-end cap to prevent the cable from fraying. This will prevent injury (the ends can be very sharp) and enable you to make further adjustments to the brakes.

08

The exact position of the saddle and handlebars relative to the pedals is one of the things that makes your bike yours. Adjusting the seat and controls to suit you can take time, but you'll ride more comfortably, and faster, for longer. It's well worth spending some effort on.

FITTING AND ADJUSTING THE SADDLE

There are several types of seat post cradle and most good-quality posts have a one-bolt fixing. This means that the cradle will be removable and easy to rebuild. Saddles now have cut-away sides and this makes it much easier to access under the rails and fit the top cradle. Seat posts with dual bolts are very secure but harder to adjust. I like these because they tend to stay put and are less likely to make a noise or rattle loose as some single-bolt seat posts can.

1 To adjust the saddle angle, loosen the post at the back bolt. Then the front bolt (here with a knurled nut so it can be done by hand) can either be tightened to point the nose of the saddle downwards, or loosened to point the nose up.

2 Use a Bondhus round-headed Allen key to access the bolt to the rear of the post, which requires tightening at an angle – this prevents scratching the post and allows a full rotation of the bolt.

3 If the seat post clamp has serrations, make sure that these are clean and thoroughly degreased. Here, the black oxide indicates an area of friction where the cradle has been ridden loose and has started to wear.

4 Clean the insides of the clamp. Dry off and wipe with a light oil. Don't use grease on the saddle clamping area.

5 Single-clamp seat post bolts need lubricating around the wedges and spacers – again, use a light oil.

6 The threads also benefit from some lubrication, although make sure that any excess lube (grease can be used here) is cleaned off, as the seat post is in direct line of the rear wheel and all the road grime is attracted to the clamp area.

7 Remove and clean carbon fibre posts regularly. Use a bike polish that can buff the post to a shine

8 Clean the inside of the seat tube. You mustn't grease carbon posts – so, if the frame is tight fitting or in poor internal condition, you may well be better off with an aluminium post. If you must fit a carbon post, seat tubes can be reamed out to clean up the insides and prepare them.

9 Make sure that there are no sharp edges and burrs inside the seat tube, and that the seat post collar is undone, before trying to insert the carbon post. Scratches in the surface of the lacquer (like these shown here) are OK as long as they're below the insertion point – deep scratches and gouges are not OK. Any damage to the surface layer of carbon means that the post should be replaced immediately.

10 If you're using a carbon post, fit a saddle collar like this Campagnolo one. This prevents the collar from binding up around the back of the seat tube slot and damaging the post. If you have a standard seat collar, you can turn the collar around so that the slots are opposite one another. Damage in this area can be catastrophic, so be careful.

11 Only tighten to manufacturers' recommended torque settings. If your post still slips, don't keep tightening it – the chances are that you need a different-diameter post or your frame needs attention. Over-tightening carbon posts can crush the post's tube, so be careful. Carbon assembly paste can help with slippage.

FITTING AND ADJUSTING HANDLEBARS

There's a simple test for checking your handlebar position – take a look at your handlebar tape. Where is it most worn? On the tops? Behind the brake levers? Or on the drops? Many riders hardly ever use the drop part of their bars, usually because they're too low and too far away to be used comfortably. Handlebar choice can play a great part in getting comfortable, so select the bar that has the right reach, width and drop, as riders generally use bars that are too big in all these dimensions.

1 Handlebars should be positioned in the stem carefully – aim to keep them as scratch-free as possible. When installing them, take care not to twist them in the stem too much, as this can scratch the surface of the bar, which creates a stress riser and can fail at a later date.

2 There's usually a mark or series of marks on the bar where the centre section is. This will also give you an idea of the preferred angle of the bar. Line this up with the front cap of the stem.

3 The flat ends of the bar should be at the bottom of the bend, either parallel with the stem or the floor. Round bars usually need the flat part pointing towards the axle of the rear hub. When fitting new bars, establish the right riding angles, and that the drop position is feeling natural and comfortable, before you start to add the brake levers.

▶

4 To fit the levers, first remove the clip from the rear of the lever – don't try to push the lever on with the clip still attached, as it'll only scratch the surface of the bar (especially important with carbon bars).

5 Slide the clip into position – they're a snug fit so should hold their position OK. Some bars have a rough section behind the bar at the lever position to add grip and indicate the point to position the lever.

6 All makes of lever (pictured is Shimano) have a recessed 5mm Allen nut inside the lever housing, which attaches to the bolt trapped in the lever clip. It helps to pull the rubber hood back a little to locate the lever housing over the bolt.

7 On Shimano this can be accessed via a channel on the outside of the lever hood.

8 SRAM and Campagnolo levers require the lever hood to be rolled forwards (be careful not to rip the hood as you pull it over the thumb lever on Campagnolo levers). Use a T-bar Allen key to access the nut on these types.

10 The controls can be positioned parallel to the ground – use a ruler to line them up with the flat top section of the bar. Don't over-tighten them, as the levers' clips can easily break. Levers can also bend if they're not allowed to move a little in the event of a crash.

9 Line the tip of the brake lever up with the base of the bar (flat section) – use a ruler and get this approximate before trying different hand positions to get the feel right.

11 Make sure that you can comfortably reach the brake levers, wrapping your fingers around the lever to get full leverage. Ergo bars (with a straight section on the drops) don't always allow this, especially for riders with smaller hands.

HANDLEBAR TAPE

Clean bar tape gives your bike a lift and it's best done after a good service (or stripdown). Each mechanic has their own way of taping bars so none can be described as the textbook method. Like any finishing touch, it's all down to taking your time and being prepared, choosing the right tape and making sure it's the last job you do on the bike. Wash your hands and have everything at hand, as you do need to have both hands free to do this job properly.

Getting the tape smooth is the priority, but you want to make sure there are no bits uncovered. Overlap the tape by a third with each wrap – this will vary according to where you are on the bend or flat section, but always check that the bit you are covering up hasn't got creased underneath. There is nothing more distracting than a lump under the bar tape.

Judging the "pull" on the end of the tape comes down to experience, and the tension should be increased a little if the sticky backing is no good. A good bar wrap needs to be tightly wound – however, pull too hard and you risk ripping the fabric.

1 First, strip off any of the old tape and any tape or debris stuck to the bars. Clean the surface of the bars, as the sweat penetrates the tape and can make the bars a bit greasy and unpleasant. Use an alcohol-based cleaner or citrus degreaser. Clean off any residue and dry off completely. Fix the levers in place (see previous pages for details).

2 Pull the rubber lever hoods away from the bars and fold them inside out (be careful as you can rip them). This allows clear access behind and means that the underside can be wrapped easily.

3 Then tape the control cables in place with electrical insulating tape (make sure that the controls are correctly aligned first). Unsecured cables will help unravel the tape, and spend some time making sure that they are long enough and don't need replacing.

5 Campagnolo Ergopower levers require both gear and brake cables to be wrapped under the tape. Most handlebars have a groove rolled into the section so the cable can recess slightly and remain comfortable to hold.

4 Some mechanics wrap the whole top section of bar so that the cables don't "drift" under the tape – it's essential to secure the cables this way under the tape so they will be out of the way when you start applying the top layer of tape.

6 There are grooves at the front for brake cables and at the rear for gear cables. If there is a separate channel for gear and brake cables and you are using Shimano levers, you can add a filling section (use a cut strip of the old bar tape) into the rear channel so that the tape will be smooth and round on the back when wrapped up.

▶

7 Bar tape usually comes with an extra short section to be curled around the back of the brake lever clasp and fittings. Cut this so that it can cover the back of the bar around the brake lever. (On Campagnolo Ergo levers this may need to be angled slightly, as the lever body is a little longer than Shimano.)

9 Continue to wrap the tape around, angling it so that the overlap will cover the next wrap of tape, especially around the bend, until you get two turns from the lever. Judge how many turns it will take to reach the lever and cover the bar and the levers without a gap, and adjust the overlap slightly to get to this point.

8 Decent cork tape is sticky backed so it stays in place, and this may be protected with paper backing. Peel a little of the backing off (not all of it at once, as you may stick it to itself, a bike part, the cat, etc). Start at the open end of the bar with the end of the tape at the underside of the bar and work from the inside out, and leave three-quarters of the width of the tape to overlap the end of the bar.

10 If you approach the lever at the right angle, you can take the tape around the back of the lever and over the top of it once, which should cover the section and both sides of the lever in one turn. This can be influenced by the shape of the bar and the position of the levers.

11 Here we have gone around the back and over the top of the lever, but this may mean you have to give it a couple of goes to get it right. Try repositioning the short bit underneath so that it helps cover the bits the tape misses.

12 The section on the top of the bar, just behind the brake lever, is the section that gets the most wear, so pay careful attention to getting the overlap here consistent. Any gaps, "under-lapped" bits or creases under the tape here will cause you all sorts of bother later. Take your time to check underneath the bar too.

13 The back of the brake levers should be double checked too, as this is your last chance to get this right before starting the finishing touches. The back of the lever should be properly covered. If there are gaps, undo the section and redo it, but be careful to unwrap the tape slowly, as you can rip it easily in frustration!

14 The final run of tape goes almost all the way to the centre of the bar. Where the centre section starts, there is usually a rise in the diameter. Unravel the last wrap and cut a straight edge from half-width to the front side of the bar. Cut a wedge shape away so it matches the angle of the wrapping.

▶

15 For a smooth centre section, wrap the final turn around and behind the brake cable where it will tuck in smoothly. Once the end is finished off straight, wrap this up with a single thickness of insulating tape.

16 Leaving three-quarters of the width of the tape to overlap the hole at the start allows you to finish the bar end plugs neatly. Stuff the excess into the bar end by folding the ends of the tape into the open end of the bar. Crease the tape like this so that it maintains its position before inserting the end plug.

17 Then force the end plugs into the bar ends. They should push fit fairly easily – if they are very tight, trim a little of the excess off and try again.

18 Lastly the rubber lever hoods will cover up the mess under the lever, but overlong covering pieces underneath will make the hood lumpy, so trim them down to the bare minimum and tape them into place with some electrical tape. Keep the bulk under the hoods tucked away or removed.

FITTING PEDALS

1 Before you start, remember that pedals have a left- and right-handed thread. Most systems stamp "L" and "R" on the axle somewhere so you know which is which. On Shimano pedals, this is stamped on the flat part of the pedal spindle, where the spanner attaches.

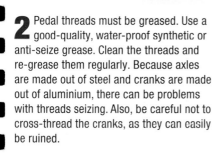

2 Pedal threads must be greased. Use a good-quality, water-proof synthetic or anti-seize grease. Clean the threads and re-grease them regularly. Because axles are made out of steel and cranks are made out of aluminium, there can be problems with threads seizing. Also, be careful not to cross-thread the cranks, as they can casily be ruined.

3 Left- and right-hand pedal threads tighten up in the direction of pedalling. The easiest way to remember this is to hold the pedal up to the crank, flat on your fingers, and spin the cranks backwards as if you were freewheeling.

4 Some pedals have Allen-key fittings, and these usually require a long Allen key to either tighten correctly or, more importantly, provide enough leverage to remove.

5 Tighten the pedals to the manufacturer's recommended torque setting. Hold the opposite crank or the rear wheel and use the added leverage to help you tighten the pedals.

6 To remove the pedals, it's probably easiest if you stand the bike on the floor. You'll remove the pedal in the direction of the freewheel, so you may have to hold the opposite crank to prevent it from spinning.

7 If you're using clipless pedals for the first time (and they have tension adjustment), back the springs right off, so that the release tension is minimal. This helps getting used to the system and enables you to get out easily to put your foot down. Over the first few days you can tighten them.

8 As Speedplay pedals are double-sided, they're a lot easier for first-time users – there's no need to flip the pedals to step into them. The cleats are the spring-and-release system.

FITTING AND ADJUSTING PEDAL CLEATS

Once you've installed the pedals, you can fit the cleats to your shoes. Most shoes use the three-bolt system, which makes it easiest to set the angle of cleat and retain a solid fixing for the step-out flick. Make sure that the bolts are the right length and don't protrude into the sole.

Look to align your feet in the way you walk. Foot alignment is becoming a very serious business and most good bike-fitters will now recommend that you see a podiatrist to get custom-made footbeds, which provide stability and align your feet for more efficient pedalling. The pedal axle needs to be directly under the ball of your foot, so spend time and get it right. Regular cleaning and lubrication are essential. Always pick out any of the jammed-in mud and grit from around the cleat, as it can prevent stepping out of the binding.

Walking in road shoes wears the cleats out quickly and is pretty dangerous anyway. Rubber covers are available for most pedal systems, and they'll prevent slipping on hard floors and avoid wear to the cleat. Worn cleats are likely to release easily and when you least expect them to (in a sprint!).

1 Assess the position of the ball of your foot over the pedal axle. Mark on the side of your shoe where the ball of your foot is, then mark a line across the sole of your shoe. This is where the cleat will be placed. Use this reference to decide which set of holes in the plates to use.

2 Prepare the threads in the plates with copper slip. The cleats will rust pretty quickly if you don't. You can replace these screws with stainless steel bolts (you can buy these from an engineering supplier), as they're less likely to rust up and will therefore last longer.

3 Most systems have slotted washers to allow plenty of fore and aft adjustments. A light grease on these will help keep them easy to adjust.

4 Tighten the shoe cleats to the recommended torque setting. Don't over-tighten them, as the threads can strip very easily, in which case you would have to replace the sole insert. Check the bolts regularly, as they can shake loose.

5 The correct cleat position is with the ball or pushing part of your foot over the pedal axle. This requires measuring and some trial and error to get spot-on. It's also

best to get someone to help you do this job, as you can only adjust the cleat position properly once the cleats are in place.

6 Speedplay cleats have a four-bolt fitting cleat and they're supplied with a plate that fixes to the three-bolt-pattern shoe. The cleats are also the sprung part of the system and need regular cleaning and lubricating (use a very lightweight oil). The cleat bolts should be Loctited into place, as they cannot be too tight. Over-tightening the bolts will prevent the springs from moving and therefore prevent the float.

7 Time pedals now have the same three-bolt pattern cleat fitting as Look and other manufacturers. The brass cleat snaps into the pedal-binding and needs to be kept clean.

FINDING THE RIGHT RIDING POSITION

The wrong riding position can cause you all sorts of problems, in particular a bad back. Here are some suggestions to help you get it right – get a friend to help you, take photographs or use a full-length mirror to help you get the best balanced position.

SADDLE HEIGHT

TOO LOW

This will place excessive strain on the knees. Track riders and time triallists often ride lower to achieve maximum power – however, a balanced road riding position is usually for long periods in the saddle, so too low can create problems.

TOO HIGH

The rider will have to stretch to reach the pedals at the bottom of each stroke, which tilts the pelvis and pulls on the lower back muscles. The same principle applies if you bob back and forth excessively when riding hard.

ABOUT RIGHT

The knee should be slightly bent at the bottom of the pedal stroke. An easy way to judge this is to have the heel of your foot on the pedal with your leg fully extended at the bottom of the stroke, then pedal backwards. If you find that you rock from side to side excessively, your saddle is too high and you need to reset it so that you feel smooth in this position. This way, when the ball of your foot is placed on the pedal there will be a bit of extra slack built into your saddle height.

PEDAL TIPS

1   Noisy or creaking pedals can be due to worn cleats or simply dry threads. Re-grease the threads regularly and replace your cleats before they start to release on their own. It's not only annoying, it can also be dangerous.

2   If your cleats are shaking loose regularly, use some Loctite on the pedal-bolt threads, especially if you ride on cobbles!

3   The cleat will wear more quickly on the side you release most often when you stop, so swap cleats around periodically (if they're not left- and right-specific).

4   Pedal washers may be supplied with some cranks, especially carbon cranks. These are intended for use with pedals that don't have a round shoulder (usually cheap pedals) where the flats are exposed. These can otherwise bite into the crank and damage the carbon.

5   Regular cleaning and lubrication are essential. Dirty pedals become sticky to get out of and can seize completely. Never walk across mud or grass, as the muck can bung up the sensitive spring system.

6   Binding as you pedal and loose bearings are usually the telltale signs of a bent axle. Replace axles after a crash – extensive spares are usually available.

STEM LENGTH

TOO CRAMPED

This will make you arch your back and stress the lower muscles. It also means you ride with your weight further forwards, which will make the steering sluggish.

TOO STRETCHED

This usually forces you to lock out your arms and strain your neck to see ahead, both of which will contribute towards lower back pain. The handling will feel sketchy and a bit too light.

ABOUT RIGHT

A balanced position means that you'll be able to stretch out comfortably and bend your arms to assist in shock absorption. With the stem in the right position, your weight will be better distributed over the bike.

SADDLE FORE/AFT POSITION

TOO FAR BACK

This is good for climbing power and pedalling comfort over a long ride, but places extra strain on neck, arm and shoulder muscles.

TOO FAR FORWARDS

You'll get a lot of pedal power in this position, but it places a lot of stress on the larger muscles, and can cause fatigue and tightness in the upper leg.

ABOUT RIGHT

You should be able to pass a vertical line (use a bit of string and a weight for a plumb line) through the centre of your knee (the bony lump just behind your kneecap) and the pedal spindle when the cranks are parallel to the ground.

The headset is an often-neglected part of the bike, perhaps because these days it's usually hidden away out of sight. But given that you rely on smooth, slop-free headset bearings to steer, it's a good idea to take care of them. Almost every new bike comes with a threadless headset system and clamp-on stem, although there are still many bikes out there with the traditional threaded headset and quill stem.

HEADSET ADJUSTMENT AND SERVICING

The Aheadset is a very simple component and the unit is therefore relatively easy to maintain and service. The system consists of two bearing races positioned at either end of the head tube. The races run in these bearings and are trapped by the fork at one end and the stem at the other. The stem clamps the system together and prevents it from coming loose. A well-prepared head tube and a properly fitted Aheadset will help the unit last longer. Even the cheaper Aheadsets on the market can last a long time if your bike is properly prepared and the unit is serviced regularly.

BASIC ADJUSTMENT

1 To check the Aheadset, apply the front brake, and rock the bike backwards and forwards. You'll feel or hear a slight knocking if the unit is loose. If you've been running the unit loose for a while, the chances are that the bearings will need replacing – riding with a loose Aheadset will batter the bearings and ruin the surfaces in the unit.

2 It's also possible that the system is too tight or notchy. To check this, pick up the front of the bike and let the bars hang under their own weight. Stiff head parts won't budge. If the Aheadset is too tight it's unlikely that it'll flop to one side, as shown here. A properly adjusted Aheadset with smooth bearings should have no play and be able to move easily, as shown.

3 Loosen the two bolts on the side of the stem. These bolts clamp the stem to the top of the steerer and also keep the Aheadset unit complete.

4 Once you've loosened the bolts, tighten the top cap slightly (this preloads it) to take up any play in the system. You'll only need a small nip to tighten the unit (around 3Nm). If you're removing the top cap and fork as well as the Aheadset, be aware that the fork will be free to fall out once the clamp is undone and the top cap removed.

5 Retighten the stem-clamp bolts to the recommended torque setting. Always use a torque wrench to check the final time, especially if you're using a carbon steerer and/or stem.

TAPERED STEERERS

Many modern bikes have tapered steerer tubes that are 1.5in in diameter at the crown and 1 1/8in diameter at the stem, with different-sized upper and lower headset bearings. This adds some fork and frame stiffness without too much of a weight penalty. Adjustment and servicing is as for a conventional "straight" headset, but make sure you get the right type of replacement parts.

SERVICING

If you're servicing the Aheadset bearings, remove the bars and disconnect the front brake so that the forks can be removed and set aside.

1 The bearings will either be a sealed cartridge or ball bearings, as shown here. Both systems are good, but the advantage with loose bearings is that they can be stripped out and re-greased. The advantage with cartridge-type bearings is that they can be completely replaced. If the bearings are wearing out regularly, the cups could be out of line in the frame and they'll therefore need to be refitted.

2 Once you've serviced the bearings, the forks can be re-installed. Make sure that you return all the seals the right way up, and that you grease the bearings and insert them into the cups the right way around. Don't leave the forks in the bike without returning the stem, even if the friction in the seals appears to be enough to hold them in place.

3 There should be a gap between the top of the steerer and the inside top of the Aheadstem of approximately 2–3mm. The gap shouldn't be any bigger than this, as the Aheadstem bolts must be able to tighten over the steerer. If the bolts are above the height of the steerer, the stem will be distorted and won't be tightened to the correct torque figure. The problem isn't just that you might pull the bars off, but the stem will also loosen over time and damage the bearings.

4 When you replace the top cap, check that the bottom of the top cap doesn't snag on the top of the steerer. If it does, you may have to place an extra spacer on top of the stem to give a little more space.

5 Most stems have two clamp bolts, one on either side, so that the stem won't be pulled over to one side as you tighten the bolts. It's critical that you don't over- or under-tighten these bolts. Retighten the stem clamp bolts to the manufacturer's recommended torque settings – which will be adequate and will mean that the bars will still twist in the event of a crash.

6 Before refitting the handlebars, check that there are no sharp edges around the stem clamp. Also check that you have the right diameter bars and stem. Standard road stems are 26.0mm, but the latest size ("oversize") is 31.8mm. Most decent handlebar stems, such as the one pictured here, have slightly chamfered edges. Put a dab of copper slip on the stem bolts before replacing them, to prevent them from seizing.

7 Replace the front section of the bar clamp. Number the bolts 1–4 clockwise, then tighten them alternately (e.g. 1–3–2–4) and to 6–7 Nm. Don't over-tighten the bolts or tighten them too quickly – make sure you reach the desired torque setting gradually. Line the handlebars up and make sure that you've positioned them centrally and that there's an equal gap at the top and bottom of the stem faceplate.

8 Check that the bars are straight and that the stem is tight. Recheck the play – if the Aheadset remains tight and you've tried resetting the stem bolts, it's likely that one of the bearings or weather seals has been inserted the wrong way, so check this and re-tighten using a Torque wrench and the manufacturer's recommended torque settings.

THREADED HEADSETS AND STEMS

Standard headsets share similar parts to Aheadsets, especially the frame cups. Installation of the basic frame parts is the same. The main difference is the fitting to the forks and how the stem attaches to the fork.

Headset types for road bikes are fewer than for mountain bikes. Road bikes never had 1 1/8in standard-sized headsets with quill stems – they changed straight over to 1in and 1 1/8in-sized Aheadsets, with 1 1/8in taking over as the "industry standard" soon after. Standard quill stems and headsets are now rare, and while there's nothing wrong with them and they work just as well, they require some specialist headset spanners to adjust. The quill stem is less serviceable than an Aheadset, as it's harder to remove the bars without removing the tape and the brake levers. However, the best thing about quill stems is that they offer larger ranges of adjustment than the Aheadset system.

1 The quill stem is held in place with a wedge system that traps the shaft of the stem inside the fork steerer. A 6mm Allen key holds the wedge tight in the end of the stem.

2 Even after the bolt is undone, the stem stays wedged in place – don't undo the bolt completely, but just enough so that the head of the bolt protrudes from the stem.

3 Tap the top of the bolt gently with a plastic mallet, or use a piece of wood to protect the head of the bolt and use a standard hammer.

4 The quill stem system has plenty of adjustment for height, but there's a minimum-insert limit line marked and you mustn't go beyond this. It's worth noting that the height range available with a quill stem is far greater than an Aheadset system.

5 The bolt travels the length of the stem and the wedge is attached to the bottom. It's important not to undo the bolt too far, as the wedge can fall into the stem.

6 The standard 1in headset requires two 32mm headset spanners to undo the locknut. The bottom one traps the forks and prevents them from spinning, then the locknut can be removed.

7 The locknut threads onto the fork steerer, and there's a washer underneath, between the steerer and the top locking nut.

8 The top race sits directly on top of the bearings, which in turn sit inside the top cup. To service the system properly, you'll need to remove the forks and access the bearings at both ends of the headset.

9 The threaded part of the steerer has to be cut precisely. This Shimano headset has a sealed bearing unit that can be replaced. Campagnolo headsets (and Aheadsets) still use ball bearings held in cages, which can be cleaned, re-greased and replaced.

10 Adjustment is simple but requires the right tools. Once the top race has been threaded onto the forks and nipped up, the locking top nut and washer can be screwed on and into place. Balancing the play and free-running bearing is a question of tightening the race and backing it off against the locking nut.

11 Once you've finished servicing the headset, make sure that you clean and grease the inside of the fork steerer and the wedge-and-quill arrangement before you re-install the stem.

If you've followed all the advice in this book so far, your bike will be clean, well maintained and highly unlikely to let you down. You can't prevent every mechanical malady though, and sooner or later you'll need to mend something by the side of the road rather than in the comfort of your workshop.

ON-BIKE TOOLS

Most of the mechanical situations that may arise on a ride can be remedied with basic tools. Always carry a folding set of Allen keys, with a small screwdriver, tyre levers, a tube or two and a set of emergency patches. A saddle pack will carry this basic kit. You'll need a pump too – a full-size frame-fitting pump is the most efficient, but most riders opt for a mini pump either on a clip under a bottle cage or just in a jersey pocket.

For longer rides, you might want to add a chain tool, a spoke key, a small spanner and some minor spares, such as brake pads and chain links. Always leave your ride tool kit intact and keep it just for riding. Taking tools out to fix your bike at home will mean you'll leave your tyre

levers on the kitchen table and not have them when you really need them.

An alternative to a saddle pack is to stuff tools in an old water bottle in a spare bottle cage. Use a toe strap to secure it so it can't rattle out. If you're doing a big ride in a group, you can share larger tools around rather than all carrying everything – make sure you've all got the basics, though.

It's a good idea to stuff a pair of latex or nitrile gloves into your saddle pack too. They take up almost no space and you'll be glad of them if you have to tackle a messy job like mending a broken chain. You don't want to be covering your hands in old chain lube and then grabbing your fresh white handlebar tape...

FIXING A PUNCTURE ON THE ROAD

The humble puncture is the most common mechanical incident. There's only so much you can do to avoid punctures. If your tyres are in good condition and properly inflated, and you avoid debris-filled gutters and sharp-edged potholes, you're as safe as you'll get, but you'll never be immune. If you get lots of punctures, consider a heavier tyre – ultralight race tyres have very thin casings that are easier for sharp objects to penetrate.

1 Stop as soon as you realise you've got a puncture and it's safe to do so. Riding on a flat tyre doesn't do it (or the wheel rim) any good. Move off the road and remove the affected wheel (see pages 22-24). Lay the rest of the bike down somewhere safe – standing it upside-down is tempting but is likely to scuff the saddle, lever hoods and bar tape.

2 Inspect the tyre for any obvious causes for the puncture. There's a good chance that whatever made the hole – a thorn, a piece of glass, a small bit of wire from a car tyre – is still there. If you find it, pull it out. Let any remaining air out of the tyre.

3 Many tyres can be removed by hand without needing levers. Start by using your fingers or thumbs to pop the tyre beads inwards from the hooked edge of the rim. Then, starting opposite the valve, squeeze the tyre beads together and push the tyre down into the well of the rim.

4 This gives you a little bit of slack, which you can then push around both sides of the tyre, using one hand in each direction. Once your hands are halfway around, it can help to pick the wheel up and support the near edge with your hips to give you something to push against.

5 Once you've got around to the valve there should be enough slack to pull the tyre upwards away from the rim. You don't need much – to replace the tube you just need to unhook the tyre bead from one side, and once you've lifted a few inches of the bead the rest is easy.

6 Pull the tube out. Check the inside of the tyre for sharp objects – the best way to do this is with your fingers, but be careful because whatever it is is obviously quite sharp. When you're satisfied that the tyre is clear, put a little bit of air in the new tube – just enough so that it holds its shape.

TUBULAR TYRES

I always carry an old, worn, spare that has some glue already on it. If you haven't got a used spare, spread some glue on a new tyre (and let it dry off completely) so that there is something to stick to, so you can get home in safety. It's not as good as a properly glued tub, but it's better than nothing. Never ride on an unglued tyre, as this is very dangerous.

7 With one tyre bead still in place, push the valve of the new tube into the valve hole and tuck the tube into the tyre all the way round. Then work around the wheel to refit the second bead. It's a similar process to removal – get one section on, then push that into the well of the rim to give enough slack to engage the rest.

8 Check that the inner tube isn't pinched between the tyre and rim and that the bead is properly on the rim all the way around. Then inflate the tyre. It'll take a while with a mini pump and you may not be able to reach your desired pressure – "as hard as you can manage" is a good guide.

FIXING A BROKEN CHAIN

Chains can break for all sorts of reasons. Bad shifts can twist links and weaken them, although the most common cause is simply that the chain is worn out – keep an eye on the amount of wear (see page 60) to avoid this happening.

1 Regardless of the cause of a chain breakage, there are usually damaged links either side of the break. Remove this with a chain tool so you're joining straight links. This will leave your chain a little short, so be careful which gears you select afterwards.

2 It's best to use a quick-link to repair a broken chain on the road – you don't want to be faffing with Shimano joining pins. SRAM Powerlinks work perfectly well on Shimano chains. Just make sure you have one that's the right width for your chain – 9 and 10-speed chains are different. To join a chain with a Powerlink, you need to have an inner (narrow) link at each end of the chain.

3 Put one half of the Powerlink through each end of the chain and lock them together. Nine-speed links can usually be popped into place by hand – ten-speed ones may need you to use the cranks to help. See page 63 for more on using Powerlinks.

4 Give yourself plenty of slack chain to work with by unshipping it from the chainrings and gently resting it on the bottom bracket, taking care to not let it get stuck between the crank spider and frame. With the chain on the rings you're fighting against the rear mech tension when trying to join it.

OTHER REPAIRS

Punctures and broken chains are the usual maladies, but nearly everything on the bike can be fixed by the road as long as you've got tools with you.

LOOSE CRANKS

Properly-fitted cranks shouldn't work loose, but it does occasionally happen. Older square-taper cranks are fixed with 15mm bolts which you're unlikely to be carrying a suitable tool for, but Octalink and ISIS cranks have 8mm Allen bolts which most multitools will cope with. SRAM GXP cranks can be tightened in a similar way. The pinch bolts on Shimano HTII left-hand cranks can be carefully tightened with a 5mm Allen key – make sure that the plastic preload cap is correctly tightened first. See pages 66-71.

BRAKES

On long tours you should be carrying spare brake pads. Modern cartridge-style pads are easy to change, but be sure to check the pad alignment with the rim afterwards.

Sometimes brakes can become uncentred, either having twisted on the mounting bolt or because the spring tension is unbalanced. See Chapter 7 for more.

WHEEL WOBBLES

It's easy to carry spare spokes – you can tape a couple to your seat- or chain-stay. Some touring bikes have specific fittings for spare spokes. The alternative is a cable spoke, which is what it sounds like – a length of cable with a threaded section at one end and a hook at the other. They're compact and can be threaded onto the drive side of a rear hub without having to take the cassette off.

CABLES

If your gear and brake cables are well maintained, you shouldn't experience any surprise breakages. But it's worth carrying a spare of each on long rides or tours – they're light and don't take up much space. They're easy to replace (see page 86 for brake cables and page 52 for gear cables). You'll end up with a long end on the cable – coil this up out of the way and trim it when you get home.

TRANSPORTING YOUR BIKE

You have several options for transporting your bike – in your car, on a boot rack, on a roof rack or in a travel bag. Some are better than others...

IN YOUR CAR

The safest way to carry your bike is in the back of your car. Remove both the wheels (see pages 22–24) and then wrap the chain and rear mech in a cloth so as not to get oil all over the place. If your car is tall enough, put the bike upright – most aren't, so try to pack your bike last and on top of all your other kit, and lay the wheels under the frame. It's a good idea to get some wheel bags (bin liners are good too), especially if it's been wet. Try not to let the tyres rub on anything sharp, or you'll have a nasty shock when the sidewalls wear a hole and puncture.

ON A ROOF RACK

Remove all loose-fitting equipment, such as drink bottles, tool packs, pumps and so on. Fasten the front wheel into the wheel clamp. Give the fork leg a good shake to ensure it's tight. Fasten the rear wheel strap and you're set. Before you drive off, double-check that all the straps are tight and you haven't left anything on the ground around the car or on top of the roof.

If you stop for anything, lock the bikes to the rack (most racks now have lockable fork fastenings) and always use a roof rack with lockable roof brackets. Lastly, don't go into a supermarket or height-limited car park, as this will ruin your bike, car and roof rack. And yes, it does happen more often than you might think!

ON A BOOT RACK

Boot racks are not ideal. Many retro-fit to the car with straps and rest on bumpers and rear windows, and are therefore not suited to carrying heavy bikes or more than two. They scratch your car and can, in time, damage the rear windows. The best type of boot rack is one that fits to the tow bar or is a permanent fitting.

PACKAGING YOUR BIKE

If you're lucky enough to be flying somewhere to ride, you'll need to pack your bike into a bag or box. Rigid cases are the safest option, but also the most expensive. The cheapest option is a cardboard box – shops recycle lots of these so you should be able to get hold of one easily.

1 First, remove the pedals, saddle and seat post. Wrap these up in a jiffy bag and place them straight into the bag or into your hand luggage – don't leave them on the kitchen table. Remove bottle cages too, as they can get bent or, even worse, damage fragile frame tubes in the process.

2 Remove the wheels and take out the QR skewers. It's worth letting the tyres down almost completely – they shouldn't explode in the hold, but it's better to be safe. I leave a little air in just to protect the rims and to provide some more padding. Use a fork-end protector (readily available from bike shops) to protect the ends from drops and prevent the forks from being pushed inwards.

3 Cover the ends of the axle with cardboard to prevent them causing any damage inside the bag. Better still, use the plastic axle covers that the wheels are supplied with (a local bike shop should have a good supply). Use plenty of pipe lagging (insulating tubes) to protect the frame and forks. Wrap some around the forks and the cranks too, as it absorbs a lot of shock.

4 Preferably place the wheels in the bag or box and tape them to one another at the rim, or use electrical zip ties. Space them so that the cassette and axle won't damage the frame. Better still, put them in padded wheel bags too to prevent any damage to the spokes.

6 Bike boxes do protect bikes from impact, but I still place spacers in the rear dropouts and forks, just in case baggage handlers decide to run the box over... This type of chain hanger will keep the ends protected and prevent the chain from flapping around.

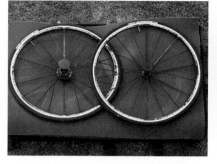

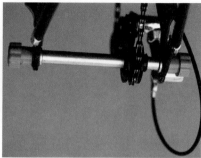

5 If you're using a padded bag, remove the rear mech, as it's vulnerable and is one less thing to be sticking out and getting bent as your bike is thrown into the hold. Wrap it up in a plastic bag along with the chain. Duct-tape it to the rear triangle, safely out of the way.

7 If you're packing your bike in a bike box, you may well have to remove the handlebars to fold the bike flat. Tighten the bolts that you've removed to prevent losing them, wrap the bars in bubble wrap, and duct-tape anything in place that could damage your paintwork and components in transit.

GLOSSARY

Aheadset – bearing unit for forks, utilising an unthreaded steerer

axle vice – device for holding axles without damaging threads

ball-peen hammer – engineering hammer with a rounded end

barrel adjuster – threaded adjuster that can be turned with the fingers

BB axle – bottom bracket axle

bench-mounted grinder – electric grinder that mounts to a workbench

bottle cage bosses – threaded inserts into frame to allow bottle cage to be attached

bottom bracket shell – the part of the frame that houses the bottom bracket bearings

bottom bracket tapping and facing kit – the tools for preparing threads and faces of the bottom bracket shell

bottom bracket threads – threads inside the bottom bracket shell

bottom brackets – generic term for the bearing and axle for the chainset

brake bridge – part of the frame for hanging the brake from

brake calliper pivots – the points on the brake caliper that pivot

brake shoes – metal-retaining parts of the brake pads

braking surface – flat part of the rim that is used to brake

cable doughnuts – small rubber grommets that prevent cables from damaging the frame and paintwork

cadence – speed of pedaling (measured in rp/m)

callipers – the brake parts at the wheel

cantilever brakes – a type of brake used on cyclo-cross and touring bikes for increased tyre clearance

captive-bolted cranks – cranks with bolts that, when undone, will self-remove the crank

carbon steerers – the fork steerer made from carbon

cartridge brake shoes – where you can use replaceable brake blocks rather than the entire unit

cassette – usually referring to the rear gear sprockets (gear cogs) it is the cluster of cogs

cassette body – the part of the hub that the cassette attaches to

cassette carrier – the type of gear system used

cassette lock rings – for tightening and retaining the cassette to the rear hub

cassette sprockets – the individual gear cogs

chain checker – device used to check the wear of a chain

chain hanger – a frame part (or additional spare part) used to retain the chain (usually attached to the inside of the seat stay)

chain tool – or riveter used to remove and replace chain rivets when breaking or replacing a chain

chain whip – a small section of chain attached to a handle, for holding sprockets when undoing cassette lockrings

chainline – the angle of the chain between front chainring and rear sprocket

chainline gauge – tool used to set or check chainline

chainstays – the two frame tubes that connect the bottom bracket shell to the rear dropouts

chainwheel or chainring – the front cog of the drivetrain

chorus groupset – a type of Campagnolo product groupset

clipless pedals – pedal system that enables the shoes to be secured to the bike without clips and straps

compact crankset – a crank with small mountain-orientated chainrings

compact drive system – the whole gear set up – cassette, derailleurs and cranks – for smaller mountain-orientated gears

cone spanners – flat spanners devised to access small spaces behind cones and lockrings

cones – conical shaped metals parts for the bearings to run in

crank bolts – bolts to hold cranks to bottom bracket axle

crank-removing tool – tool for removing cranks

cranks – the two shafts that attach the pedals to the bottom bracket axle

crankset – the collective term for the left and right crank

crown race – the headset bearing surface that is attached to the fork, at the crown

crown race remover – tool for removing said crown race

crown race setting tool – tool for installing crown race

cup-and-cone hubs – hubs that have loose ball bearings and can be adjusted

cup-and-cone systems – hubs that have loose ball bearings and can be adjusted

derailleur – device that moves the chain over sprockets (rear derailleur) or chainrings (front derailleur)

diamond pattern – the standard term for the classic frame design

dishing stick – tools used for checking alignment (dish) of the rear wheel

drive train – pertaining to the drive (gears, chain, sprockets, pedals)

drive-side cone – cone on the gear/drive side of the bike or wheel

drive-side crank – or right hand crank

drive-side spacer – spacer on the gear/drive side of the bike or wheel

dropouts – the part of the frame that anchors the rear wheel

dual-pivot brakes – contemporary design brakes with increased power through dual pivot design

ergopower brake – Campagnolo's term for integrated brake and gear levers

eyeletted rims – rims with stainless steel inserts at the spoke holes

facing tool – a tool for flattening a surface of a tube (Head tube, crown race or bottom bracket)

fork crown facing kit – tool for squaring up fork crown

fork crown race – see crown race

fork ends – where the wheel is held in the fork (can also be called drop outs)

fork steerer – the tube that attaches to forks to the head tube

fork-end protector – small plastic part used for packaging bikes

frame alignment tool – tool for checking frame alignment

front hub – central element to the front wheel housing bearings and wheel axle

front-facing dropout – a rear dropout that faces forward, so the wheel is removed towards the frame

gear hanger – part of the frame that is threaded for the rear derailleur

gear ramps – elements pressed into the gear sprockets to enhance and assist gear shifts

gear shifters – levers that change gear

granny ring – on a triple crankset it is the smallest chainwheel

head angle – angle of the head tube

head tube – frame tube that holds the forks

head tube reamer – tool that prepares the head tube for the headset fitting

headset or Aheadset – the bearing parts for the forks

headset cup remover – tubular steel tool that splits and allows the headset cups to be 'knocked-out'

headset cups – the parts that hold the bearings for the steering

headset press – tool used to push-fit headset parts (cups)

hub – the part of the wheel that holds the axle and the bearings

hub body – the main part of the hub, also known as hub body

ISIS – international standard type bottom bracket design

jig – a device for holding something while working (frame jig, wheel jig, etc)

jockey wheels – small wheels inside the rear derailleur

lacing – pattern of the spokes in the wheels

lever hoods – rubber covers that protect the hands from the brake levers

lock nut – nut that is tightened onto another part to prevent it from moving

lock rings – as above (usually bigger)

long-cage mech – rear derailleur with a long cage for wide ratio gears

mech – another word for derailleur

octalink cranks – a Shimano pattern design for fixing cranks to axle

over-shifts – where the gear mechanism travels too far with one gear shift

parallelogram mechanism – derailleurs have a parallelogram design with plates that move about pivots to change gear

Park Tools – USA quality tool brand

pawls – small metal parts that engage inside the freewheel mechanism and

make the clicking ratchet sound

pedal cleats – plastic plates that engage with the pedals to keep the rider fixed in to the bike

pedal threads – the threads that affix the pedals to the cranks

pitting – damage to bearing surfaces

play – when the bearings come loose this is referred to as 'play'

podger – a tool for poking holes

presta – high-pressure valve for racing bike inner tubes

QR skewers – the central shaft on quick release lever systems, usually refers to the complete mechanism

quill stems – a stem design from before Aheadset systems, uses a quill that is tightened into the head tube

ratchet ring – the inside part that creates the freewheel

rear dropout alignment tools – tool used to check and repair rear dropouts

rear dropouts – where the wheel is inserted and held in the frame

rear mech – or rear derailleur

record hub – top of the range hub by Campagnolo

removing cassettes – see cassettes

rim eyelet – a steel insert into the (usually) aluminium rim that holds the spoke nipple

rim hole – the hole at which the spoke is attached to the rim

saddle-to-bar drop – the distance between the top of the saddle and the centre of the handlebars

schraeder – a valve design, similar to those used on car and motorbike tyres

seat tube – the tube of the frame that the seat post fits into

seat tube reamer – a tool used to clean out the seat tube

self-centring jaws – jaws that adjust and move together independently

Shimano STI lever housings – the body that holds the gear and brake shifting assemblies

sidewall – the side of a tyre (not the tread)

skewer – see QR Skewer

soft drift – a tool that can be used to hammer sensitive parts without damage

spacers – used at the Aheadset to adjust the height of the handlebar stem

speedplay cleats – specific cleats used for speedplay pedals

spoke keys – tool devised to fit spoke nipples

SRAM Red – a pro level groupset made by SRAM

SRAM/TRUATIVE cranks – a brand name of cranks made by SRAM

star nut – small threaded widget that attaches the Aheadset top cap to the fork steerer

star nut-setting tool – tool for inserting the star nut into the fork steerer

stays – the chain or seat stays or mudguard stays

steerer cutting guide – a clamp with a slot in it for sawing the fork steerer

stem – usually refers to the handlebar stem extension that attaches the handlebars to the fork steerer

top tube – the tube that connects the seat tube to the head tube

triple drivetrain – three-ringed cranks

truing – straightening (wheels)

tubulars – tyres that have integral inner tubes stitched into them

tyre boots – larger puncture patches that can repair ripped tyres

unship – fall off (re: chains)

vernier calipers – engineers' tool for measuring

wheel dish – the shape of the wheel

wheel dishing stick – see dishing stick

wheel jig – or truing stand, used to true and adjust wheels

wheelbase – distance between front and rear wheel axles

INDEX